Bella Should Have Dumped Edward

Bella Should Have Dumped Edward

Controversial Views & Debates on the Twilight Series

michelle pan

Ulysses Press

Published in the United States by
Ulysses Press
P.O. Box 3440
Berkeley, CA 94703
www.ulyssespress.com

ISBN: 978-1-56975-822-9
Library of Congress Control Number 2010925851

Acquisitions Editor: Kelly Reed
Managing Editor: Claire Chun
Editor: Richard Harris
Proofreader: Lauren Harrison
Production: Judith Metzener
Front cover design: what!design @ whatweb.com
Cover images: © istockphoto.com/tatarnikova

Printed in the United States by Bang Printing

10 9 8 7 6 5 4 3 2 1

Distributed by Publishers Group West

To my parents, Dawei Pan and Zhiang Wu,
for their endless love and support.
Thank you! I love you both!

○○○
table of contents

ooo
acknowledgments

This book would not have been possible without the help of Ulysses Press. Thank you for giving me this fantastic opportunity!

Thanks to Stephenie Meyer for creating the wonderful world of Twilight and the story of Bella and Edward. Without you, none of this would be reality. Thank you for changing my life!

Thanks to all of the fans who submitted entries for this book, including Alejandra Marin, Alex Embleton, Alison Ng (LostinBelieving), Andrea Daembkes, Anthoula Tasioudi, Bristol Galbraith, Cynthia Serna, Dawn Atchley, Dayi Martinez, Deidre Frost, Elisabeth DeCrane, Elizabeth Rodriguez, Emily Bryan, Hannah

Severns, Haylee Voda, Kristine Velasquez, Morgan Moore, Morgan Schutterle, Nicole Hobday, Paige Davis, Rachel Hahn, Rachel Leff, Rachel LeSage, Roni Hughes, Savannah Sanford, Shannon Angelo, Shelley Morris, Taylor Gleason, and Tine Kempenaers. Your passionate debates are what keep the fandom and BellaAndEdward.com alive.

Thanks to all of the BAE staff members and forum staff for always keeping the site updated, especially during the three months of craziness when I was writing. And thanks to Robin for helping me come up with the lovely questions featured in this book.

Last, but certainly not least, thanks to my friends and family for their support and enthusiasm. I couldn't have done it without you guys!

ooo
bibliography

Meyer, Stephenie. *Twilight*. New York: Little, Brown and Company, 2005.

Meyer, Stephenie. *New Moon*. New York: Little, Brown and Company, 2006.

Meyer, Stephenie. *Eclipse*. New York: Little, Brown and Company, 2007.

Meyer, Stephenie. *Breaking Dawn*. New York: Little, Brown and Company, 2008.

OOO
introduction

I fell into the world of Twilight during the middle of 2006. It was the summer between my seventh and eighth grade years, and just like every other summer, I had a reading assignment to do. Entranced by its mysterious cover, I decided that *Twilight* was going to be the book for my assignment that year. Little did I know that "book with the apple on the cover" would change my life forever. A couple months after finishing the novel, I started my own Twilight fan website, BellaAndEdward .com, and since then it has grown to be one of the largest and longest-lasting Twilight fansites on the web.

My journey with *Bella Should Have Dumped Edward* began in the fall of 2009, three years after I was first introduced to the world of Bella, Edward, and Jacob. I was approached by Ulysses Press and asked to write a Twilight debate book similar to *Mugglenet.com's Harry Potter Should Have Died*, which they had published a couple months before. Naturally I took on the job without a second thought, only to realize later that I already had an insane workload to deal with. The next couple of months were hectic as I tried to balance school, band, and BellaAndEdward.com *on top* of writing a book. Trust me, it wasn't an easy task! But thanks to the fans who submitted their wonderful responses to many controversial Twilight questions, I was able to get some great ideas and persevere with my writing.

Speaking of fan input, let me tell you a little about how this book is organized. It all started with 30 of the BellaAndEdward.com staff members' burning questions about the Twilight saga. Should Jacob have imprinted on Renesmee? Should *Breaking Dawn* have ended with a fight? Should Summit Entertainment have replaced Rachelle Lefevre? All of these questions and more can be found in the pages of this book. I then asked for fan input on the topics, and that's when we really got the ball rolling. I was thrilled to see that fans of all ages and from all over the world were eager to participate in this project. As fans sent in their responses (some passionately defending their arguments), I quickly categorized them under the appropriate questions and proceeded to write my portion of the book. At the end of each chapter, you will find "The Final Call," my own opinion on the matter. While it isn't really a "call" and certainly not final, it does make me feel quite a bit more important! My thoughts on the question proposed sometimes adhere to the fans' opinions and other times don't. But either way, the fan responses are just as crucial to the book as my opinions are (if not more so). After all, this is a book about "Controversial Views on the Twilight Series"; if I had written the book by myself, there would only be one view and it would make quite a boring read. So my point is, I couldn't have done this without the fans. You guys made this book possible. Thank you for being such dedicated Twilighters!

After three months of hard work, here is my finished product: *Bella Should Have Dumped Edward: Controversial Views & Debates on the Twilight Series.* I do hope you enjoy this compilation of fan opinions from all around the world and share it with other Twi-hards you may know. Who knows? Maybe you'll get into a heated debate over whether Bella should have picked Edward or Jacob.

Oh, and for the record, Bella definitely should *not* have dumped Edward.

○○○
if you could be any twilight character, who would you be?

Bella Swan

Taylor, 16, Wisconsin

If I could be any Twilight saga character, I admit that I would love to be Bella. I know, so cliché, right? But even though she goes through all this hard stuff when she comes to live in Forks with Charlie, she finds love. And not just her one true love—she also finds a best friend. She has everything that I will ever want out of life. She's so lucky. I know a lot of people who just think the series is all so cheesy and poorly written, but I don't know how they can't see what Bella goes through as something exciting and amazing, even if her life is threatened on more than one occasion. If I could be anyone, it would be her. I'd have Edward all to myself and Jake as a BFF. And even though one is a vampire and one is a werewolf, having people with personalities like theirs love you makes it seem impossible that life could get any better.

Kristine, 20, Texas

Like any girl who loves the series, I would love to be Bella. Bella's life is not only exciting and intriguing, it is her own special world. Some people go through life with someone who never loves them a fraction as much as Edward loves Bella. Edward is unselfish, considerate, humorous, and a complete gentleman, among many other things. Although in *New Moon* it may seem like he is selfish in leaving her, he does it to protect her, though he is wrong, as he admits, and he apologizes for it. Bella's friend Jacob is beyond supportive. Although he hurts for almost all of the series because he loves her and she loves Edward, he is always there for her, as well. Like Edward, Jacob avoids Bella when he turns into a wolf because he doesn't want to hurt her. That shows how much she is loved. Not only would I want to be Bella because of how loved she is and how romantic her relationship with Edward is, but because she is a modest, genuine girl. She is not materialistic in the slightest and is an example to everybody who reads the series. She has a big heart and puts others before herself, even to the point of putting herself in danger. If life as a vampire with Edward were at stake, she would turn into a vampire in a heartbeat.

Alice Cullen

Sarah, 25, California

I used to want to be Bella. I think it was because she's the main character and she has this wonderful man who loves her so much that he would gladly lay down his life and happiness to save her. Recently though, I have found myself drawn to Alice. She is so caring and kind, and like Edward, she would risk her life to save Bella. Alice is also compassionate and optimistic, which makes even the direst situation seem manageable. She has one of those relationships with her mate, Jasper, that isn't complicated. They, too, are soul mates, but they don't have all the angst and pain that accompanies Edward and Bella's relationship. Alice seems confident and self assured, never doubting herself. That is someone I would strive to be every day until I accomplished my goal. She's the first one to accept Bella even though she's a human. That shows me she isn't prejudiced and is willing to keep an open mind. Alice is fiercely loyal, brave, and strong, which can make her a force to be reckoned with when her family is in danger. Most of all, I would want to be Alice because she is graceful, with a classic sort of beauty, but her heart outshines anything that is only skin deep. It is her heart and soul that ultimately make her ultimately, and I would rather be told I have a beautiful soul than a pretty face.

Esme Cullen

Deidre, 22, Alberta, Canada

I would want to be Esme because she has such a good, kind heart and cares deeply about her family and Bella. She just wants the best for everyone, and she doesn't seem to be angry about being a vampire. She realizes that it is what it is, but she has a wonderful man who loves her and children to care for who love her back. She's a strong woman and isn't afraid, and that makes her a great character.

Renesmee Cullen

Savannah, 14, California

I would want to be Nessie. She is a unique girl because she's a hybrid. She also gets imprinted on by an attractive, fun-loving werewolf. Her family is huge and consists of vampires, werewolves, and humans. They all love her and care for her so much. To be her would be absolutely amazing. She has an amazing power and will get to live forever but still grow, at least for a while. Her mother and father are deeply in love with her and each other, which just shows how much love there really is in the world. Nessie also seems like a very bright, independent person. I would pretty much give anything to be her. It seems like she has the perks of being a vampire, like speed, strength, and special powers, without having the uncontrollable thirst for blood. This seems like a good life to me. Plus, it is almost completely unexplored, so there is no right or wrong way to live it.

THE FINAL CALL

Which Twilight saga character would you want to be? Bella Swan, right? Many Twi-hards would agree, saying that Bella has it all, with a vampire boyfriend, a werewolf best friend, and on top of that some normal human friends too! Bella's boyfriend is madly in love with her, and he is willing to do just about anything to protect her. But while it's easy to say every girl wants to be Bella Swan (who doesn't want Edward Cullen as a boyfriend?), a good handful of fans lean more toward other characters, like Alice, Esme, and even Renesmee.

Alice has the personality, the confidence, and the ability to see the future. She's the kind of person that, according to Stephenie Meyer, is loved by both the girls and the guys. Esme, a compassionate, strong woman, embraces the fact that she is a vampire. She cares for the entire Cullen family and opens her heart to Bella as well. Renesmee is a unique case. She has the best of both (actually, three) worlds, being half-vampire/half-human and having a werewolf as her lifelong companion. Renesmee is surrounded by love from not only her parents, but also from her extended family and Jacob Black. And as Savannah pointed out, Renesmee's life "is almost completely unexplored, so there is no right or wrong way to live it." So in the end, which Twilight character's shoes do most fans want to be in? The majority of fans landed with Bella Swan because she is surrounded with people, vampires, and wolves that care for her, and she reciprocates that affection in her life.

○○○
who is the best character in the twilight saga?

Renesmee Cullen

Paige, 16, Texas

Renesmee is the best character in the Twilight saga. Each character is different, especially because some are vampires and some are werewolves. But Renesmee is something unique: She is both human and vampire. Every reader knows that her kind is special, and that is why she is the best. She has this ability to live a different and fulfilling life. Renesmee is also connected to Jacob, which is the last piece of the puzzle that ties all the characters together. She is an amazing person who makes the story end on the perfect, settling note.

Rosalie Hale

Deidre, 22, Alberta, Canada

I think the best character in the Twilight saga would have to be Rosalie. She shows a negative side to being a vampire and really shows that it isn't all that it is cracked up to be and it isn't easy. She may treat Bella horribly throughout most of the saga, but you learn that she had a good life going for her until it went terribly wrong, and I think anyone who went through that wouldn't exactly be the most pleasant person afterward. Eventually you see a more caring and nurturing side of Rosalie. She is more of a human because of the emotions she displays—more than any other character, I believe.

Carlisle Cullen

Haylee, 17, New York

The best character in Twilight, in my opinion, is Carlisle. Even though the books and movies aren't centered around him, and the movies are even less so, you still manage to get a sense of his good heart. Edward looks up to Carlisle throughout the entire series, and he acts like a *real* father to all of his "children." Edward's admiration for Carlisle is so clear in every decision he makes.

The fact that Carlisle has never killed a human being really says something about the kind of character he is. Instead of staying a "monster" like every other vampire in their world, Carlisle has guided himself and his family to only consuming animal blood. Carlisle is also a doctor and has almost become immune to the scent of blood and manages to give back to his community and help people. He is a truly compassionate, loving, and caring person.

Anthoula, 31, Athens, Greece

Although I absolutely adore Edward Cullen, the best character for me in the Twilight saga is Carlisle. Carlisle is the Cullen that keeps the rest of the family sane and helps maintain their balance with their bad vampire side. Carlisle was the first of the Cullens that got into his vampire life and had to learn how to fight his most violent and repulsive instincts. He decided to be different and create a new way of life without hurting humans and living peacefully among them. It was not easy at all for him since he had no one to teach him or help him find his own balance. It took him a lot to manage it, but that's how he became the cornerstone of his family, a father figure for them, and a good husband for Esme. He is always the one who stays calm and in control, assesses the situation, and organizes the rest of his family to reach whatever their goal is.

THE FINAL CALL

The best character in the Twilight saga ... this is a tough question to answer. While you would expect most fans to automatically say Edward Cullen, that actually wasn't the case here. A handful of vampires (surprisingly, no werewolves) were nominated: Renesmee, Carlisle, and even Rosalie. Now, you might question why anyone would pick out Rosalie, but Deidre from Alberta, Canada, gave a pretty solid reason to justify her thoughts. Rosalie contrasts the other vampires in the Cullen family by showing the "negative side to being a vampire." She shows more emotion and is more human than the others in the clan.

Even so, I have to say that I believe that Carlisle, who is not my *favorite* character, is the *best* character in the series. He was the one who built and laid the foundation for the Cullen family. Carlisle made the choice to be a "vegetarian" vampire and throughout the years he changed and converted others to his cause. The Cullens would not exist without him; he is the father figure and backbone of the family. Carlisle Cullen also provides a crucial service to the population of Forks. Being the town's only doctor, Carlisle assumes a great responsibility in taking care of the people. He overcame a vampire's weakness to blood to assist others in need. That's the sign of a truly compassionate and selfless character.

○○○
which twilight
saga book is the best?

Twilight

Paige, 16, Texas

The first book, *Twilight,* is the best out of the entire saga. It is the basis for the whole story. Everything that happens in that book is what makes the relationship between Edward and Bella flourish. *Twilight* sets the characters up for the rest of the series, and all the details give the fans information about what is in the other books. The story is also very intriguing as readers see everything progress. After you complete the series, you see connections that were established in the first book recur in the other books. These are things that do not seem obvious until you finish the whole saga.

Bristol, 17, Texas

While *Breaking Dawn* has the most plot twists and gripping action, *Twilight* still has the number-one ranking. *Twilight* was written without complication: there is Bella, the average protagonist that everyone can relate to, admire her intelligence, and identify with her clumsiness; there's the protective father, Charlie, that has that awkward an connection with his daughter that just makes him adorable; and then of course there is the modern Mr. Darcy, Edward Cullen, who cannot help but mesmerize women into falling in love with his old-fashioned charm, chivalry, and stunning looks. *Twilight* has an unpredictable, engaging plot, but also lets readers form their own opinions. *Twilight* introduces an entirely different world that invites readers in so they will never want to return to reality.

Dawn, 26, California

The first book is by far the best because it demonstrates the give-and-take that has to occur in order for Bella and Edward to become an item. The reader is allowed to view the courtship of Bella and see through her eyes why Edward Cullen is romantic and every young girl's fantasy. It also sets the stage for the reader to fall in love with Edward and their relationship, despite the apparent cruelty that takes place in the second book.

Eclipse

Rachel, 15, Georgia

The best Twilight saga book in my opinion is *Eclipse*, which has the Bella, Edward, and Jacob love triangle at its peak and truly shows us the benefits of each side before letting Bella come to a decision. *Eclipse* is probably also the most exciting, with the werewolves and the war with the army of newborn vampires. *Eclipse* tells us of the joys that could come from Bella and Edward's relationship without the pain of conclusion that comes from the end of a series.

Deidre, 22, Alberta, Canada

Eclipse is the best Twilight saga book because it explores some characters' back stories so you get insights into why they are the way they are. There is also the love triangle in which Bella really realizes her feelings for Jacob and starts questioning things. It also shows that Jacob and Edward both really care about Bella so much so that they are willing to stand together in the fight just to save the woman they both love. *Eclipse* sets the relationship between werewolves and vampires that becomes even more intense in *Breaking Dawn*.

Rachel, 14, Illinois

A hard question in and of itself. I think that the Twilight saga, as a whole series, is written to perfection. Though, if I were forced to chose, I would say that I enjoyed reading *Eclipse* the most out of the four books. In *Twilight,* not that it wasn't a good book, but it felt almost like a prequel for the dramas that were coming. *New Moon* was also a very good book, yet I felt like it was more a book that Stephenie Meyer wrote to take us further into Bella's mind and emotions. *Breaking Dawn* was a great, completely unexpected way to finish the story, bringing us to the absolute edge of immortality and showing us exactly how strong Bella really is.

In *Eclipse,* we see a different side of almost every character we thought we knew before this book. We see Bella pushing herself closer to the breaking point emotionally and making decisions that change everything. We see Edward wishing and waiting for Bella, yet trying to give her freedom and ultimately showing his willingness to let her have whatever and whomever she wants. We see Jacob Black as almost an enemy to Bella at points in the story, confusing us about their friendship in *New Moon*. At the end of *Eclipse*, Bella has made her decision, choosing who to let go and who to hold onto forever.

Breaking Dawn

Roni, 12, Birmingham, England

I think the best book is *Breaking Dawn*. So much happens that you just can't put it down. You just have to know if Edward comes through on his promise to Bella, if Bella really is pregnant, and if the wolves kill Bella. It's so much more addictive than the other books. Even though the ending is a bit disappointing, the rest of the book makes up for it!

Cynthia, 14, Texas

For me the best Twilight book is *Breaking Dawn* because it involves Bella and Edward going to a higher level, such as getting married and having a baby. During *Breaking Dawn* many things occur, and Bella gets transformed into a vampire during the birth of their daughter. The only issue is that instead of going straight to a happily-ever-after, they have to face the consequences of Bella's health and the Volturi. It's like you ask yourself, "Will the Cullens have a happily-ever-after?" or "Will the Volturi get between them?" Only the reader can answer that question. *Breaking Dawn* involves a lot of things that nobody has seen before, like a newborn vampire/human child who's a few weeks old and a werewolf imprinting on a newborn child. How weird can things get? It involves the vampires and werewolves teaming up together to save their family. Also it includes many new characters that you never heard of, or had heard of but just hadn't gotten the details about. In *Breaking Dawn*, you get to experience whether or not the characters get a happily-ever-after.

Can't Decide!

Emily, 17, Georgia

I can't decide between *Twilight* and *Eclipse*. I pick *Twilight* because it introduced everything, a different world and everything. I also pick *Eclipse* because it explored more of the relationship between Edward and Bella and Jacob and Bella. We were also given background stories on Rosalie and Jasper. The whole vampires vs. werewolves background was also explored, along with the continuance of Victoria's revenge on Edward and Bella. I loved how the vampires and werewolves joined forces against Victoria's army. The action of *Eclipse* really had that "can't put it down" pull, for me anyway. Plus it had the official proposal to Bella from Edward.

THE FINAL CALL

Let's start from the beginning. *Twilight* is where the story starts. It was the book that drew everyone into the story of Bella and Edward, the book that started it all. Surprisingly, *New Moon* was not a popular choice; could it be the lack of Edward for the majority of the novel? *Eclipse* seemed to be the all-fan favorite. Twi-hards favored the third novel because of its action, its back stories, and because it is, in a sense, the climax before *Breaking Dawn*.

In *Eclipse*, the stories of Jasper and Rosalie are revealed, giving us a deeper understanding of why the characters act the way they do. We also see Bella, Edward, and Jacob's relationships develop and come to an climax as Bella contemplates her choices. Finally, *Eclipse* is when Edward's official proposal to Bella occurs and the two become engaged.

In *Breaking Dawn*, fans are led on a journey, as Bella marries Edward, has a baby, and battles through the hardship and uncertainty that follows. There are so many unexpected plot twists in *Breaking Dawn*, and every page turn brings a mood of suspense. As Cynthia pointed out, readers are kept on the edge of their seat as they ask "Will the Cullens have a happily-ever-after?" or

"Will the Volturi get between them?" My personal favorites from the series are *Twilight* and *Breaking Dawn,* but most fans prefer *Eclipse* over the other novels.

which twilight
saga book is the worst?

Twilight

Anthoula, 31, Athens, Greece

Not the worst because it is necessarily bad, but because
it is the first, the *Twilight* book is the "worst." Stephenie
had never written anything before the first book of the
saga, so her writing skills here are pretty raw. The idea
is perfect, but since it was the first, it has all things in
chaos. In the movie, Melissa Rosenberg put things in
order and brought the book into balance for the screen.
Sure, you enjoy a book more on your own time, and her
writing conjures beautiful images in your head, and she

creates characters we love, but everything is rough as far as writing is concerned.

Another reason is that it is the beginning of the story and we just get acquainted with the story and the characters. Just when things start to get exciting, we are at the end of the book and we have to move to the next book of the saga to enjoy much better writing and have the real story begin and get into the excitement of their everyday problems and all the dangers that lie ahead. So for me the main two reasons are these: rough writing skills, so the story is a little all over the place and chaotic, and the lack of serious excitement other than meeting the characters and getting to know them, which of course is unavoidable. So, for me it is the weakest link of the saga and not the worst in the true sense of the word.

Roni, 12, Birmingham, England
Twilight is the worst book, in my opinion. Yes, the first time you read it, it's gripping, compelling, romantic, and you don't want to put it down. But once you've read the rest of the series and you go back again, *Twilight* is kind of boring. Bella doesn't know anything, so there are no vampire issues. There is no Jacob, so there are no fights, and Bella and Edward don't do anything. There is no romance, not like in *New Moon* or *Eclipse*.

New Moon

Emily, 17, Georgia

New Moon, not because of the lack of Edward (because I am a huge Edward fan), but because of the lack of life. Bella's in a depression and can't move on, which everyone will experience once in their life. It's completely understandable not to be social or friendly for a while, because everyone has to work through getting over someone on their own time. The fact that the book seemed to go on and on about how she missed him and loved him and how she lived her life seemed to stretch out the book day-by-day. It took her four months and Charlie threatening to make her go to Jacksonville to actually try to go out with a friend and try to get her mind off of it, even just for a few minutes. It would've been healthier for Bella to hang out with her friends every now and then instead of doing nothing for months at a time. She could've held on to the memory all she wanted, but I would've found it more enjoyable if she'd let herself get her mind off Edward for a while.

Eclipse

Dayi, 19, Georgia

All the books are wonderful in their own way, but if I had to choose, I would say that *Eclipse* is the worst book in the saga. I did not like how much Bella's physical weakness was emphasized, especially when she punched Jacob after he kissed her and it did not bother him at all. I also didn't like Charlie's support of the unwanted kiss. Even so, Jacob Black's heartache was probably the worst of the book. Regardless of the fact that it was completely necessary to have him hurt a little, it is still hard to watch a character—who is loved despite his many flaws—suffer that much. Not to mention how much it must have tormented Edward when Bella realized she was in love with Jacob and kissed him. I was somewhat disappointed that Bella was in love with two people because it was always a belief of mine that one person could not possibly love another person the right way if he or she were in love with someone else. However, Stephenie Meyer showed me the light!

Breaking Dawn
Rachel, 15, Georgia

Breaking Dawn is the worst Twilight saga book because of its spectacular buildup and very annoying letdown just before the conclusion. Parts of *Breaking Dawn* almost seem cheesy, and not the kind of cheesy we've come to enjoy from the other Twilight saga books. When Bella compares her life to the Fate's Loom, I nearly groaned at how silly she made herself seem. Also, Bella and Edward's transition to parenthood seemed too smooth to be believed, even if they did have the perfect baby.

Deidre, 22, Alberta, Canada

I wouldn't say that any of the Twilight books were horrible, but I do believe that maybe some of what happened in *Breaking Dawn* could have been edited down or maybe had a different result. I really enjoyed the first half of *Breaking Dawn,* but halfway through, it became harder for me to follow and really enjoy reading. It just became very confusing, with people coming and going, and I sometimes had to go back and reread parts just so I understood it better.

Alex, 17, London, England

Whilst I enjoyed all of the books, I found *Breaking Dawn* the worst, as it seemed to get more and more unbelievable whilst the character development didn't seem to be well established. I found the way Rosalie almost seemed to want Bella dead so she could have Bella's baby disturbing. At the same time, Rosalie was so supportive and friendly to Bella that one didn't know quite what to make of the situation. The use of Jacob's persona was a nice change, but I felt it left the reader out of the picture to some extent and emotionally detached from Bella in her time of need. In addition, I felt that the ending was also slightly sickeningly sweet and in many ways seemed too perfect. Finally, I found the image of Bella drinking blood through a straw and Edward's pillow biting a tad odd and too laughable.

Rachel, 23, Saskatchewan, Canada

The absolute worst book of the series is *Breaking Dawn*! It was a horrible read and too long, with both bad story and character arcs. *Breaking Dawn* should have been an incredible buildup, climax, and ending to the books, but instead it fell short, went off track on a completely weird tangent (i.e., grotesque birthing scene), and utterly alienated itself from the three previous books. *Breaking Dawn* is nothing similar to the other books, and it also has a poorly written ascension of the plotline to a complete failure and utter disaster of a "climax" and ending of the four-book story line. My honest question is, how can a story with that many vampires on opposing sides, randomly pumped into the plot, manage to have everyone survive in the end? I understand that writers can do whatever they choose, but it takes away from the sincerity and believability of the characters just so that the writer can have a "happily ever after" fairy tale ending. I know this is a fantasy novel, but the writing is trying to make it real for each reader. Unfortunately, in reality not all of your beloved characters survive such a formidable battle. The creation of Renesmee, Bella and Edward's daughter, produces such an ideal and perfect character that she is ultimately unrealistic and unbelievable. In my opinion, she too severely disrupts the story arc of Edward and Bella as a couple by taking them into immediate parenthood. I absolutely hate that Jacob imprinted on Renesmee too—very weird story line! *Breaking Dawn* had so much discontinuity from the previous three books that I felt the connection was lost between the characters I had gotten to know. The only way to "save" *Breaking Dawn* is to have a second version of the book and to steer clear of the failures within the book to stay true to the essence of the story line—no Renesmee and no unbelievable fairy tale endings!

THE FINAL CALL

To my surprise, an overwhelming majority of fans named *Breaking Dawn* as the worst book of the Twilight saga. The last installment was actually one of my favorites, along with *Twilight*. Fans say that the events in *Breaking Dawn* were too unrealistic and that the ending was disappointing. I have to agree with the latter, but I personally don't think the plot was hard to believe. Fans have already been sucked into a world of vampires, werewolves, and supernatural powers, so what's so unrealistic about a half-vampire baby? For me the worst book would have to be *Eclipse*. It felt like Stephenie Meyer was using the book to prepare readers for the final novel rather than have it tell its own story. I think it's necessary for each book in a series to lead to the next, but I felt that *Eclipse* lost its personality in the process. Every other book in the series has a main plot point. In *Twilight* Bella meets Edward, in *New Moon* Edward leaves, in *Breaking Dawn* Bella has a baby (among many other things). While *Eclipse* was a good story, I felt it was lacking a major plot point. I was also annoyed by Bella's personality in the book. Between Jacob, Edward, and her confused emotions, she was just a mess. I did not enjoy the lack of a unique plot or Bella's instability in *Eclipse*.

ooo
which movie was a more accurate representation of the book: Twilight or new moon?

New Moon

Rachel, 15, Georgia

Although I adored both movies, I believe that *New Moon* was a more accurate translation of the book, mostly because no major details were left out. *New Moon* covered basically every scene and plot point that was in the book, while *Twilight*, for cinematic reasons, skipped quite a few. *New Moon* also had more direct or almost direct quotes from the book. And with a bigger budget, the director could make the costumes, make-up, sets, and special effects almost exactly in synch with the book.

Paige, 16, Texas

New Moon portrayed the book more precisely than the *Twilight* movie did. I feel like *Twilight* left out some important scenes that I have would loved to see acted out. Despite the movie having to leave some things out to meet a time requirement, some scenes (such as the vital meadow scene) could have been more elaborate. In *New Moon* they did a better job than in *Twilight* of showing the feeling of the relationships between Bella and Jacob, Bella and Edward, and Jacob and Edward. They also included the little details that I believe are significant to the story. Everything was brought more to life in the *New Moon* film than in the *Twilight* film.

Taylor, 16, Wisconsin

I believe that *New Moon* was a better translation from the book to movie screen than *Twilight* was by far! I actually didn't like *Twilight*'s director after I'd seen the deleted scenes from the movie: there was Victoria, who was all over James' bare chest, and then Bella had that dream about yanking Edward into bed with her. I didn't like those scenes, and even though they were deleted, they were still too wildly off base to be even filmed. I don't understand why the director even thought that those might make it in. *New Moon*, on the other hand, really only has minor changes from the book to the movie. It has almost every detail in there, and the acting, in my opinion, is more pulled together. I loved every second of *New Moon* and cried more than enough the two times I saw it in theaters. It was such an awesome movie. Chris Weitz did an excellent job!

Deidre, 22, Alberta, Canada
I really believe they were both good representations of the books. I do believe *New Moon* was better; however, I think that is due to the popularity of *Twilight*. The cast and crew also had a lot more time and money to make *New Moon* look as good as it could possibly be. The story of *New Moon* is also a powerful emotional roller coaster, so they needed to make sure they brought that to life properly. If *New Moon* wasn't made properly, it would just throw the rest of the saga off and could even set up the other movies for failure.

Andrea, 21, North-Rhine/Westphalia, Germany
New Moon was definitely a more accurate representation of the book than *Twilight*. Chris Weitz took great care to include all the crucial moments and story lines

and altered hardly any scenes (and when he did, it was with good cause). The movie portrays perfectly Bella's depression as well as the essential differences between her relationship with Jake and with Edward, which is an important setup for *Eclipse*. *New Moon* is incredibly emotional and gut-wrenching, and you are really able to understand the characters' feelings, especially the beautifully done break-up scene between Edward and Bella. The small alterations, such as the e-mails to Alice or Bella's visions of Edward, all serve to improve the movie and translate Bella's feelings and thoughts to the screen without constant use of a voiceover. The one criticism I would make of *New Moon* is the adaptation of the chapter "Truth," where Bella realizes that Edward has really returned to her. I think this is one of the most crucial chapters of the book, and I was somewhat disappointed to see it reduced to a tiny dialogue in Volterra and an even shorter one back in Forks. Apart from this, however, I believe that Chris Weitz has done a brilliant job bringing my favorite book of the series to the big screen.

Twilight, on the other hand, strays much further from the book. Granted, the first movie must be more difficult to film, and the budget was nowhere near as high as for *New Moon*, but in my opinion, Catherine

Hardwicke's movie misses the point of the book. The book is mostly about the growing relationship between Bella and Edward, about Bella's self doubts and the incredibility of someone like Edward falling in love with her (and vice versa). All those difficulties are omitted in the movie, and their relationship does not differ too much from that of any other teenage couple. Bella seems much too sure of herself and apparently does not feel all that overwhelmed by the fact that Edward wants to be with her.

Perfectly unnecessary changes were made in the *Twilight* movie, such as letting Bella realize that Edward is a vampire only after she spent the evening with him in Port Angeles, moving the talk Bella and Edward have about him being a vampire from Port Angeles to the forest (which is a pretty dreadful scene anyway), or reducing the central chapter of the book, the scene in the meadow, to a few shots of Bella and Edward lying around in the grass.

The whole relationship between the two of them seems to progress much too fast in the movie, from "I want to kill you and we shouldn't be friends," to "I'm a vampire and totally in love with you," and then immediately to "Okay, so we're together forever then." It seems as if the movie does not have an actual focus, the way the book is focused on the growing relationship or the way *New Moon* is focused on Bella's desperation.

I don't want to sound as if I think *Twilight* was a horrible movie—it had some really great moments as well—but *New Moon* is simply a lot more true to the book and overall a much better movie than *Twilight*. I'm not saying that every movie based on a book should be an exact translation of the novel to the screen, because some scenes just don't work in a movie the way they would in a book, but I appreciate the effort some directors go to in order to find a middle course, staying true to the book while still making an attractive movie—like, for example, The Lord of the Rings trilogy or, for that matter, *New Moon*.

THE FINAL CALL

Most Twi-hards will agree with me when I say that *New Moon* was a more accurate representation of the book, hands down. In the *Twilight* movie, some critical scenes were shifted and others taken out completely. Bella and Edward's first kiss, which should've happened right after the meadow scene (*Twilight*, page 282), was moved ... to Bella's bedroom. And speaking of the meadow scene, the movie, as Andrea from Germany put it, reduced the "central chapter of the book ... to a few shots of Bella and Edward lying around in the grass." It was such a shame, because Chapter 13 was everyone's favorite chapter. And what happened to the biology scene with the blood typing (*Twilight,* page 95)? On top of that, a lot of things were added that weren't originally in the book. For example, an entire character (Waylon Forge) was put in just so he could be killed off by the nomads. On the same subject, the marina scene with Waylon and his boat was also inserted into the movie. While I understand the purpose of the additions, they made the *Twilight* movie stray away from the book. In *New Moon*, Chris Weitz did a much better job of knowing what to cut and what to keep in. The plotline was very similar to that of the book, and anything that was changed did not significantly impact the overall movie.

○○○
should summit entertainment have replaced rachelle Lefevre under the given circumstances?

No!

Rachel, 15, Georgia

Rachelle was one of my favorite actors in both *Twilight* and *New Moon*. She is a great actress and truly inhabits the character Victoria in the films, almost more than any other actor becomes their character. She obviously made a mistake taking on another film that conflicted with the scheduling for the *Eclipse* shooting, but to fire her so quickly for a ten-day overlap seems quite selfish of Summit, as if they couldn't wait to even talk to her before releasing their statements.

Rachel, 14, Illinois

Under no circumstances, ever, should *any* of the actors playing vampires have been recast. The situation with Rachelle Lefevre was very unfortunate, yet totally avoidable. When Summit recast Rachelle, we were all kind of thrown for a loop. We've spent two movies getting used to this actress playing Victoria, and her representation of the character was *the* representation. Rachelle was Victoria in our minds. Did Summit not get the memo that vampires *don't* change? Now, I think that Summit did a very good job when in recasting her, as far as looks are concerned, but can this actress pull off the impersonation we've all come to know and love? Only time will tell. I feel that Summit made a poor decision when in recasting Rachelle at all, and both she and Summit should have worked harder to make each other's schedules work out.

Deidre, 22, Alberta, Canada

I do not believe they should have recast Rachelle Lefevre. The fans all know Victoria is Rachelle, and to take the hard work she did and just basically rip it out from under her and her fans was incredibly cruel. She really believed she would be in the three movies and it was extremely unfair that she wasn't able to return. I personally don't see anyone other than Rachelle as Victoria, since she was in the first two films and did a great job.

Emily, 17, Georgia

This goes both ways for me. Although I hated that they released Rachelle from her contract, finding it stupid that they couldn't work around the *ten days*, Rachelle *really* should've let Summit know about the other project earlier than a week before filming *Eclipse*. But, I think they should've kept her on for *Eclipse* since it's Victoria's last appearance in the Twilight saga, and Rachelle would've done a more than excellent job with finishing her role as Victoria.

Alex, 17, London, England

Whilst I can see Summit's reasons for recasting, I feel that a lot more could and have been done to resolve the issues surrounding Rachelle's breach of contract. From comments made by Rachelle, it does sound to me like Summit made a snap decision about recasting her, which is a real shame as she has come to represent the image of Victoria that many fans have in mind when reading the books, just as Taylor has become Jacob and Robert has become Edward. I also feel that it ruins the consistency of the films and worry about the impact of Victoria's sudden change in appearance will make when watching the films together.

Dayi, 19, Georgia

I believe that they should neither have recast Rachelle Lefevre nor even thought about doing so. Considering the craze of the Twilight fandom, I'd say it was pretty darn inconsiderate. I am not going to pretend that I know how the movie business works, but I do know how the fans think, being one of them myself. When a character is recast after we have gotten used to him or her, it takes away a certain something. Rachelle was Victoria. It's as simple as that. In my mind that was *the* Victoria, and it should have remained that way. The story sort of loses credibility when characters are recast. I believe that if they cared about the fans' feelings like they should have, they would have waited for Rachelle Lefevre before moving on with whatever it was they felt they had to do immediately. I have nothing against Bryce Dallas Howard, and Rachelle is not exactly a favorite actress of mine, but when it comes to the Twilight saga, I like for there to be constancy. All that is left to say is that I am glad they are using a good actress and that it was not a major character that they replaced with someone new. Do what you must, Summit, but please, for all our sakes: no more recasting!

Anthoula, 31, Athens, Greece

By all means, Rachelle should have been cast again and reprise her role as Victoria. Summit has in their hands one of the most loved and successful projects in the film industry at the present time, but they sometimes do some dangerous moves without careful thinking concerning the Twilight saga, and the whole situation with Rachelle has been one of them. Fans of the saga, including me of course, were totally surprised and stunned when during summer vacation they read on web that due to a shooting schedule conflict, Summit did not find a way to have Rachelle included in the *Eclipse* movie. Rachelle was more than just Victoria, she absolutely loved the whole project and the fans and appreciated their love, she was present almost everywhere to show her support and her love back to the fans. She was part of it. It was not just another role for her, as you could clearly see. Cam Gigandet had some similar problems, and they moved the ballet fight scene to the beginning of shooting, and that was at the very beginning, before the even more tremendous love after the movie was out, so I am sure they could have found a way to agree on a mutual decision to fit in both Summit and Rachelle for the sake of us, the fans.

THE FINAL CALL

Since even before the start of the Twilight movie craze, Twi-hards were trying to fit actors and actresses into Twilight roles. When it was announced that Rachelle Lefevre was to portray the evil vampire Victoria, everyone was excited. After the first movie premiered, it was confirmed—Rachelle Lefevre was the perfect Victoria. Unfortunately, after two movies as the redheaded nomad, Rachelle was taken off the cast by Summit Entertainment due to a ten-day scheduling conflict. All the fans who responded felt that this was a very unnecessary move. Couldn't they have worked out some kind of agreement to get around ten days? Apparently not. Rachelle Lefevre *was* Victoria in the minds of the millions of Twilighters who saw the first two movies. She did a wonderful job on the role, and she was always so enthusiastic to meet fans and be a part of the craziness at the various conventions she attended. Plus, *Eclipse* is the last time fans get to see Victoria, and it would've been Rachelle's final appearance in the Twilight saga had she been allowed to stay. Now fans have to get used

⭕⭕⭕
which Twilight saga movie character is most accurately cast?

Taylor Lautner as Jacob Black

Dawn, 26, California

Jacob is probably most accurately cast character in the films. The fact that the producers had Taylor Lautner almost double in size for the role perfectly exemplified the way the book describes the physical change in Jacob. In the movie, Lautner also portrays the shyness of Jacob Black in *Twilight* and then easily transitions into a more confident, prominent character in *New Moon*. I wasn't sure any one actor could pull off the transition not only in appearance but in personality as well, but I think Lautner did an exceptional job.

Alison (LostinBelieving), 14, New Jersey

All of us have different views on each and every cast member and character of the series, like who did better in this area, whose acting was horrible, and other things that we fans argue about. I think that Taylor Lautner portrays Jacob Black in a way that no other actor out there could have possibly imagined. At first glance, I knew he was born for the role.

I honestly cannot view the characters in my mind when I read the books. My friends have their own pictures of each and every character in the books, but I'm that one in a million who just doesn't picture them. I fill the blankness in with a picture of the actor or actress that ends up playing that character, if the book gets turned into a movie. But even I can just tell when an actor or actress reminds me of a character. With Taylor, I just knew. I'll admit that in the first movie, *Twilight*, his acting was a little awkward. But even he was just growing into the skin of a character that would take the hearts of millions of girls (and a few guys) everywhere.

Honestly, I hate his wig. It annoys my friends and me so much, but it fits him. With the wig, he looks like the young, innocent boy who helplessly starts crushing on

Bella. When he finally takes the wig off for *New Moon*, you can tell that both he and the character change. It shows how Taylor adapted to his character, becoming less awkward with his acting. But it also shows how Jacob changes—how the sweet, innocent boy Bella loves turns into a rough, dangerous monster he never wants to be.

Before all the physical changes he made to his body, I still thought Taylor would make the perfect Jacob. After he got the muscles, he looked even better for the perfect Jacob (if that's possible). But I'm not saying he is the most accurately cast just because of his stunning looks; I chose him because he looks and acts like the character I see when the text of the book comes alive.

Every time I see Taylor on screen portraying Jacob, I see him growing more and more into his character. The way he speaks the words is the way I picture Jacob saying them. His actions are also a major contributor. Jacob is more dangerous and daring than Edward, and I imagined him more sarcastic and carefree. The smallest expressions on Taylor's face define Jacob as the other person Bella cares for in her life. Bella likes Jacob for a reason, and Taylor definitely brings that reason to Jacob.

Robert Pattinson as Edward Cullen

Rachel, 15, Georgia

Rob Pattinson as Edward is most accurately cast because not only can Rob act like Edward in the films, he also delved into the character through research and studying in his real life. Robert Pattinson brought Edward to life in a way we could barely have dreamed of when we read the books. Pattinson makes him intense and vampirelike when he needs to be and can just as quickly go to funny and charming. The chemistry between Bella and Edward is amazing, and when you watch the Twilight films they are literally what was in your head while reading the books because of the stellar performances by the two main characters.

Anthoula, 31, Athens, Greece

The Twilight saga movie character most accurately cast for me is Edward Cullen. First of all, the physical description of Edward matches exactly that of Robert Pattinson. In the book, Edward is described as a young man of incredible beauty, boyish body figure, and perfect characteristics similar to Greek statues. That is also said about his facial characteristics when we read about his marblelike, strong, cold lips every time they touch Bella's skin. Edward is also described as a soul in emotional pain, falling in love with Bella who is a human and thus the perfect meal for him. At the same time, he has to constantly fight his thirst for blood, so good and bad fight within him, and he is also very sensitive, which makes things even worse because he finds no purpose for his vampire life. The point is that Robert shows all those powerful feelings perfectly every time Edward speaks or does not speak at all, the way he moves, and the way he acts around others and specifically Bella, so for me Robert is the perfect fit. Although I understand he knew nothing about the character before the movie, with time and hard work he found the perfect way to bring our incredibly dreamy Edward to life on the screen. I read that they had a tough time finding the perfect Edward, and that the role of Bella was a lot easier, but I cannot possibly ever imagine how Robert would lose the part, because physically and emotionally he is our Edward 100 percent.

Cam Gigandet as James

Deidre, 22, Alberta, Canada

I truly believe that they cast almost every single character really well. With that being said, the *most* accurately cast character, I believe, is Cam Gigandet as James. I think Cam really got into the character of James, realized what James is all about, and gave it 100 percent. Cam is very good at playing darker roles such as James, so he really makes you believe the character. He also scares you a bit, and James is supposed to do that.

Peter Facinelli as Carlisle Cullen

Alex, 17, London, England

Peter, not only because I feel he matches the physical description of Carlisle perfectly, but also because the aura produced by Peter on film is one of power, yet of calm control and understanding. He is able to seamlessly slip between father figure, doctor, and loving husband whilst maintaining the perfect level of continuity. In more intimate scenes, such as in the scene with Bella at the end of her birthday, he captures the intensity beautifully without it being overdone.

Ashley Greene as Alice

Haylee, 17, New York

When I think of Alice Cullen, I see Ashley Greene. Every little detail I see in Alice just came to life when Ashley Greene was cast. The hair, the sense of style, and the same joyous personality are all perfectly represented with Ashley. Alice is a fun, adorable, and all-around caring, happy person. It is sometimes hard for me to distinguish between the two of them! Ashley may bring everything I imagined Alice to be, but she also brings a little fire to her character, some sassiness that Alice didn't originally have.

THE FINAL CALL

When it comes to the cast, I'd have to say that the role of Alice was definitely the most accurately done. I didn't know who Ashley Greene was when it was first announced that she got the role of Alice, but when I saw her picture I knew she was the *perfect* match. Stephenie Meyer describes Alice as "pixielike, thin in the extreme, with small features" (*Twilight*, page 18) and Ashley Greene (despite not being 4' 10") fits the description pretty darn well! She has a very friendly face with small, pixielike features, and she brings Alice's bouncy personality to life when she's in character. Other popular choices among the fans were Taylor Lautner as Jacob and Robert Pattinson as Edward.

◯◯◯
which twilight saga movie character is least accurately cast?

Kristen Stewart as Bella Swan

Rachel, 23, Saskatchewan, Canada

Kristen Stewart as Bella is the least accurately cast character, I would say. When reading the books, particularly the first book, *Twilight*, Bella feels so tangible she could be your next-door neighbor. In anticipation for the first movie to hit theaters, I was expecting an actress to portray Bella with such meticulous accuracy to not only the description of Bella but also her mannerisms and nature. I expected to see Bella come to life from the pages of *Twilight*. Kristen Stewart appears to force the emotion and character of the Bella the readers know and recognize from the books. For example, Bella is naturally clumsy, but on film Kristen appears quite together for most of *Twilight*, except for a small moment of what seems to be a "clumsy" slip on the ice in front of her house. Kristen portrays Bella not as she is but as a blend of Bella mixed with herself and her own reactions, emotions, and mannerisms.

During *New Moon*, Kristen tries to portray a scene where Bella becomes upset and emotional when Edward breaks up with her. The emotion feels forced and unnatural. I do not connect with Kristen's Bella on screen the way I felt Bella's emotions through the books. It appears that either Kristen is trying to portray an emotion she has no idea how to convey to the audience or she has no understanding of the emotional aspect of the situation. I feel that Kristen is only acting a *version* of Bella and not who Bella truly is within the story. Unfortunately, watching Kristen Stewart as Bella, I feel that I will never see the Bella from the books, whom we all connected to and have become emotionally aligned with, ever truly or accurately portrayed on screen.

Nikki Reed as Rosalie Hale

Rachel, 15, Georgia

Nikki Reed as Rosalie is the least accurately cast role in the movie. In the books, Rosalie is described as pale, blonde, very thin, and drop-dead gorgeous. Although Nikki Reed is a very pretty girl, she is tan and brunette. With all the wigs and makeup she uses in the movie, she just can't pull off the drop-dead gorgeous look I imagined when I first read Rosalie's description. Why the director didn't cast a tall, blonde, skinny actress (and G-d knows there are plenty of them out there) is probably because the director, Catherine Hardwicke, loved working with Nikki Reed on the movie *Thirteen* and wanted to work with her again. If only actors and actresses could be cast on physicality and acting ability instead of paycheck and personality.

Dawn, 26, California

Rosalie was the least accurately cast. I think the actress who plays her should have been stunningly beautiful, with the kind of beauty that transcends race, hair color, and physicality, for example Jessica Alba or Halle Berry. It didn't necessarily have to be one of these women, as the character had to be blonde, but she should have been played by a woman whose beauty is appreciated by every person who sees her. The actress who plays Rosalie is pretty, but her appearance is nothing spectacular. The Rosalie in the book sounds almost majestic in her beauty, whereas the Rosalie on screen has beauty that only appeals to some.

Jamie Campbell Bower as Caius

Deidre, 22, Alberta, Canada

The actors chosen for the characters were good choices, except that I would not have cast Jamie Campbell Bower as Caius. I just pictured someone older in his role, preferably someone who is around the same age as Michael Sheen and Christopher Heyerdahl, because when I think of those three (Marcus, Caius, and Aro) I think of someone who is older, with more wisdom, and someone who could bring more life experience to the role.

THE FINAL CALL

This question was a tough one because all the actors and actresses that were cast are good at what they do. They can all act, but the problem is they all have their own individual styles of acting, and some of them weren't suited to be in a vampire romance like the Twilight saga. The fans had a variety of opinions on this topic, and mine is that the least accurately cast character is Bella Swan. Kristen Stewart is absolutely gorgeous, with her sharp features and model-esque looks, but Bella Swan isn't supposed to be. I've always imagined Bella as a girl with very soft features and a very bland and washed-out look, and Kristen Stewart is far from bland! Her genre is more of the indie, punk-rock scene rather than teenage love stories. I agree with Rachel from Saskatchewan, Canada, when she says that the emotion portrayed on screen by Kristen seemed a little forced. As a result, we didn't get to see a lot of emotion come out of her as Bella went through hardships and transitions in her life. Kristen Stewart is a good actress, but Twilight is just not her genre.

○○○
which character's story would make the most interesting prequel?

Edward Cullen

Deidre, 22, Alberta, Canada

Edward's story would make the most interesting prequel. It would give us a greater idea of how he dealt with becoming a vampire and living his years before he met Bella. I think it would be cool to see what he did and who met along the way. It would be also nice to see his family dynamic pre-vampire and to see his relationship with his parents so you could get a better sense of why he might be the way he is.

Anthoula, 31, Athens, Greece

For me, the character that would make the most interesting prequel, without any doubt, would be Edward. We know Edward as a vampire, and we have no idea how he was in his human life, how he grew up, how he was as a young man in 1918, or what his teenage life was like as opposed to how Bella's life as a teenager is today. I'd like to see how his parents were, the difficult times he went through losing them and almost dying himself, his meeting with Carlisle, his transformation, and eventually how he managed to adapt to his new way of living.

Edward has a very sweet, sensitive soul, and it must have been terribly unbearable for him to get used to his vampire life and find a balance between his bad side and the new way of living as a vampire that Carlisle wanted him to be part of. He had no choice in this new life, and going through that without his biological parents must have made it even worse. I would love to see how he managed to overcome his initial negative feelings and somehow find his place in a new loving family with Carlisle and Esme as his foster parents and later with his new brothers and sisters, with whom becoming close was not always as easy as expected.

Taylor, 16, Wisconsin

I think Edward's story would make a very interesting prequel because he's been alive for so long! It would just be really, really cool to be able to see what his life was like before he met Bella and then watch him change into the vampire she helps him become in the Twilight saga. Edward Cullen is my favorite character from the series (big shocker there, huh?), and it would be so much fun to see him on his rebellious streak, and then to watch him come back to Carlisle and Esme, and to see him gain each of his new family members. It makes me excited just thinking about it. I want to read more about Stephenie Meyer's world. Wow...she's such a genius.

Jasper Hale

Rachel, 15, Georgia

Jasper's story would make the most interesting prequel because so much happened in his life before he found the Cullens. A former Civil War general, he becomes a vampire, develops a power, fights in many newborn wars, gets depressed and walks away, tries to find himself, finds his true love, and finds the Cullens. Any one of these topics alone would make for a good book, and all of them together would make for an epic one.

Carlisle Cullen

Shannon, 29, South Carolina

It would have to be Carlisle since he was the one who started things in motion in the first place. He was the one who changed everyone except for Jasper and Alice. I would almost say Alice would make a good prequel, but she doesn't remember any of her past. Carlisle can start with his father and how he was chasing vampires, and then go into how he changed the rest of them and maybe a little more about his and Esme's relationship. We don't hear as much about Esme and her story as we would like to, so that would be a great way to make her presence felt more.

Paige, 16, Texas

I believe Carlisle Cullen would have an intriguing prequel. Because of his age, he witnessed a lot of history, and he was also the originator of the Cullen family. He is the reason that we have the entire series. But also to see how he became a vampire and how he officially met Esme would be interesting. Carlisle also lived with the Volturi, who we know little about even though they hold such a prominent position in the vampire community. The book would be intriguing and fulfilling because of everything that Carlisle participated in.

Esme Cullen

Roni, 12, Birmingham, England

I think either Esme or Alice would make a good prequel. Although we find out a bit about Alice in the series, there's a lot we don't learn. Who was her mother? How did she end up in the asylum? How did James find her? With Esme, all we know is that she committed suicide because her baby died. How did he die? It would be interesting to find out if she had wanted kids when she got pregnant. Did she grow to love the baby so much that it broke her heart when he died? More of her background could be interesting. I've always pictured her as having a troubled childhood with an abusive father, so she vowed to look after her kids properly.

Rosalie Hale

Elizabeth, 21, Pennsylvania

Rosalie Hale's story would make the most interesting prequel. We know that she was raped, beaten, and killed by her fiancé, Royce, and his friends, which led to her to become a vampire. Instead of focusing on her brutal past and becoming a vampire, the prequel could focus on how she met Emmett and how their relationship started. Yes, Rosalie saved Emmett from a bear because he reminded her of her friend's son, but did she ever intend on falling for him? I know that after the change they were rarely apart and were thought to be soul mates, but it would be interesting to know the details from her point of view. Did she ever have doubts about Emmett because of her ruthless past relationship with Royce? Or what about the struggles they went through with Emmett's thirst, because Rosalie has never tasted human blood, and how she coped with it? It would be exciting to get an insight on Rosalie and Emmett's "weddings" and their life as newlyweds when they lived away from the Cullens. Overall, the most compelling part of the prequel would be the complete insight of her views on being a vampire and how she struggles with not being human or able to have children.

THE FINAL CALL

I've always found myself wondering about Carlisle Cullen's long history of almost 400 years. We get to know a little about Carlisle's past in *Twilight* (*Twilight*, Chapters 15 and 16), but the stories are all told through Edward, a secondary source. Although we know the basics of how Carlisle became a vampire and how he ended up in America, a few chapters are not enough to fill 400 years of history, especially if vampires are involved! There's just so much about Carlisle that could be elaborated on, and that can only be done through a first-person prequel about his character. We would get to experience his emotions, his instincts, and his thoughts, all firsthand. How hard was it for him to control himself when he first changed? What were his experiences in Wisconsin, Ohio, and Chicago? What were his thoughts and feelings toward each new member of the Cullen family? How has he changed since his human life? A prequel on Carlisle would answer all of these questions and give Twilighters a better understanding of the leader of the Cullen family.

○○○
which character's story would make the most interesting sequel?

Renesmee Cullen

Rachel, 15, Georgia

Renesmee's story would make for an intriguing sequel. It would be interesting to see how her life progressed after having been born with a perfect match waiting for her. Another interesting plotline would be how the wolves interacted with her. Would they accept her as Jacob's imprintee even though she is half-vampire? I would also like to see how her life with Jacob worked out romantically in the end.

Roni, 12, Birmingham, England

I think Renesmee's story would make a good sequel. It could go through her life with Jacob. Maybe they have kids, even though she's half-vampire. It would be fun to see how Edward and Bella react as she falls more and more in love with Jacob (cue a few tedious moments!). I wonder if anyone would ever tell Nessie just how in love Jacob was with Bella before Nessie came on the scene, and how she would react if she knew!

Shannon, 29, South Carolina

It would have to be Renesmee. Although that wasn't my favorite part of the story, since she is around now, maybe we can see a little bit more of Edward and Bella from her perspective and how the whole half-vampire/half-human thing turns out. We know that she does eventually stop growing, but does that mean she can die as a human would? Does she face more danger than the others? Why is she not venomous? There are a lot of questions that could be answered by her. But Edward and Bella definitely would have to be a vital part of that story. Oh, and we can't forget Jacob. How does their relationship evolve? Does Renesmee end up loving him like he loves her? And what happens with his and Bella's relationship since they were once in love too?

Leah Clearwater

Rachel, 14, Illinois

At the end of *Breaking Dawn*, every single character had a happy ending except one. Leah Clearwater was left alone, unhappy, and somewhat forgotten by all of us as we cried our eyes out for Bella and Edward's long awaited happily-ever-after. In *Breaking Dawn*, we dive into Leah's head along with the rest of wolf pack and find out that there's much more to Leah than the scowl that appears on the surface. Sam has emotionally ripped her apart and left her bleeding, however unintentionally he did it. She's forced into Sam's head, and occasionally his emotions, and she is close to being pushed over the edge. When Jacob breaks away from Sam's pack, Leah follows him in a desperate attempt to get away from Sam. She finds a friend in Jacob and tells him things she's never told anyone. When Jacob imprints on Renesmee, Leah's pushed to the side again and slowly sinks into the shadows of our minds. We forget her pain and loneliness. From what I've read of Stephenie Meyer's writing in the Twilight saga, she doesn't just leave someone without a happy ending. There's got to be more to it. Leah can't just be a lonely character left in pain for the rest of her life.

Dayi, 19, Georgia

I know that I would love to hear more about Edward and Bella, or definitely Renesmee and Jacob's story. But one can pretty much guess what would be in their future: happiness, family, love, and perhaps children. The person whose story I would love to read—and find out if she ever gets her happy ending—is Leah Clearwater. Ah, Leah ... She seems hard to love, but like most, she has reasons for her bitterness. She is afraid that she would never be able to have children or that she is, as she puts it, a "genetic dead end." I would love to see her have her happily-ever-after, to read about her imprinting on her soul mate, and to watch her overcome the bitterness she cannot help but feel over Sam Uley's "betrayal." A good idea would be to write a book just about the wolf packs and their stories.

THE FINAL CALL

We got an almost half-and-half split on this question. Some fans said they would like to read more about Renesmee and her life with Jacob, while others wanted to delve into Leah Clearwater's future. As Rachel from Illinois pointed out, "at the end of *Breaking Dawn*, every single character had a happy ending except one," and that one was Leah. The fans got to know the real Leah and her story toward the end of the series, only to be left with an unfinished tale. Leah is left bitter and alone, and no one knows where her life is headed. On the flip side, Renesmee and Jacob's story ends on a happy note, but that is just the beginning. Renesmee has her whole life (with Jacob) in front of her, and who knows where that's going to go? I would love to read about how Nessie is accepted in the vampire, werewolf, and human worlds as she grows older. How will she respond to her parents' and grandparents' history? Renesmee is truly a unique creature, and to read about her future with Jacob would be a real treat!

○○○
would you rather be a vampire or a werewolf?

Vampire

Dayi, 19, Georgia

Both supernatural creatures have their advantages and disadvantages, but I would choose to be a vampire over being a werewolf or shape-shifter. The reasons are these: vampires are awesome, powerful, sometimes have extra abilities, and live forever. To be more specific, I guess vampires seem less vulnerable to me, even though that is not always true. However, I would love to have an extra ability added to the strength, speed, and magnified senses. I'd love not being affected by outside temperatures; not having to worry about (human) food, sleep, or shelter; and being able to retain lots of information. Sure I'd have to repeat high school, move around a lot, and drink blood, but I think I could make some sacrifices in exchange for being virtually invulnerable and fabulously beautiful. Besides, who wouldn't want to sparkle?

Alex, 17, London, England

Vampire, definitely. Firstly, you wouldn't have the issues of ripping your clothes every time you turned into a wolf or of being completely bound by an imprint. As a vampire you also wouldn't have to share your most intimate and private thoughts or have to put up with the unpleasant thoughts from the rest of the pack, not to mention having to obey the alpha wolf. You also wouldn't sleep, so you could get so much more done, and if you fell in love with a human you would be able to turn them so they wouldn't die and you could be together forever. Plus you get to sparkle in the sun and dazzle people with your beauty!

Werewolf

Deidre, 22, Alberta, Canada

I would rather be a werewolf for the simple fact that they are incredible protectors. For the most part, they are able to find the loves of their lives and enjoy happy, fairly normal human lives. They eat regular food just like everyone else, so they don't have to try and pretend to fit in with society. Also, being able to be warm all the time would be better than being cold.

Savannah, 14, California

This is a very, very hard question. I love both "species" so much. The vampires are appealing because of their speed and amazing beauty. In the first book we see them as perfect, like there's nothing wrong or hard about being a vampire, but having to control the thirst would be very difficult. The transformation is what scares me most. Three days of unbearable pain. Of course, at the beginning you would be going "Yes! I'm going to be a vampire!" But I know that ten minutes later I would be begging for death. And I would never be able to see my family or friends again. My friends and family are a huge part of my life, so this would be very difficult for me. If I were to be a werewolf, I could still see my friends and family. I could run extremely fast and never get hurt. Plus, I would get to turn into a wolf. You would never get cold, you wouldn't age for a very long time, and the only hard part would be when you first turn into one. It isn't unbearable pain, just very emotional. I believe that's a good circumstance, at least compared to how bad turning into a vampire is. I wouldn't have to move or give up anything besides my spare time. That sounds pretty good to me!

THE FINAL CALL

Whether you're Team Edward or Team Jacob, actually being transformed into a vampire or werewolf is totally different from rooting for one. When asked if they would rather be a vampire or a werewolf, most fans sided with the wolves. Why? Because the pain of being transformed into a vampire, the thought of staying frozen while watching your loved ones age, and the thirst for blood are all too unbearable. And fans would enjoy staying warm all the time. Overall, werewolves are more human than vampires will ever be. They won't be stuck at a certain age forever and they can still eat normal human food.

All that said, I would still rather be a vampire. Werewolves have a sort of binding "contract" with their pack. They must obey the alpha wolf and they are forced to incessantly listen in on the other pack members' thoughts. Plus, the whole imprinting thing just creeps me out. At least vampires have some control over who they fall in love with. In addition, vampires have all the time in the world (literally) to perfect their skills and learn new things. They don't need sleep, they don't need food, and technically they don't even need to breathe. With vampirism also comes a set of special abilities: super strength, speed, and your own unique talent. In my opinion, the Cullens lead a near-perfect vampire lifestyle. They have each other for love and support, and they choose to not feed on humans. As for the pain, of course it would be excruciating for the first few days, but I think it's worth the benefits.

OOO
which vampire special talent is the most useful?

Alice's ability to see the future

Elisabeth, 24, Illinois

Alice's talent is definitely the most useful. For starters, it solves a lot of money issues when you can predict stocks. To live the lifestyle that the Cullens live takes money. And moving from place to place does not give you as much of a chance to build up credentials for a high-paying job. There are other expenses, such as forged documents, to take into consideration as well. And not only is her talent useful in having money to live on, but it makes her a superb fighter. Being able to predict your opponent's next move is a fantastically useful skill in a fight. And of course, that is only if a fight actually happens. Being able to see a fight coming means the possibility to avoid it, or at least delay it, before it even starts. Alice's ability also gives her a chance to decide whom to place her loyalties with. Seeing that you are meant to end up with someone or supposed to trust someone would make life a little easier. Also, it gives you the advantage of seeing future enemies and those that would mean to bring you harm.

Alec's ability to remove all senses

Rachel, 15, Georgia

The vampire talent that's the most useful is Alec's ability to remove all the senses from his victims, and his victims are unlimited in number. Although this gift may not be as potent as his twin sister Jane's gift is, he can attack more than one victim at a time, unlike Jane, making his talent much more useful on the battlefield.

Jasper's ability to control emotions

Deidre, 22, Alberta, Canada

I think the most useful vampire special talent is Jasper's ability to calm and control emotions. It isn't easy to be living your life as a vampire and resisting the natural vampire urges, so to be able to control emotions is a great asset. It also isn't something you have to explain to people. You can just do it and people will never know. Also if you are able to control emotions, you can help control stress so everyone leads a less pressured and happier life.

Bella's "shield"

Emily, 17, Georgia

From what I've gathered from Carlisle and the Volturi, there are special known and unknown talents that certain vampires have. It seems to depend on how the person was in their human life. As for the known talents of the Twilight saga, I've got to say the best is Bella's shield. I love my privacy, so to be protected from mind readers and possess enough strength to protect loved ones from danger would really be a great benefit.

Aro's ability to read minds

Morgan, 17, Iowa

The most useful vampire special talent is Aro's mind-reading ability because with one touch he knows everything another person has ever thought and experienced. From that one touch he can see what someone values most and what their greatest weakness is. It is the most useful and dangerous talent because knowing people's weaknesses with one touch gave Aro more power over everyone in the series, and no one could get information like that on Aro. I think that if any other vampire had this power instead of Aro, the other person would be enforcing the vampire laws. I have always thought Aro's mind reading is the most interesting power in the series because I have always wondered what others have experienced.

THE FINAL CALL

Fans seem to have many different viewpoints on which vampire talent is most useful. Some say Alice Cullen's ability to see the future, because it gives an advantage in fights and financial issues; others would rather go with Jasper's ability to control emotions. My personal favorite (and the most useful in my opinion) is one that wasn't even mentioned: the classic mind-reading powers of Edward Cullen. For me, the ability to read minds has always been fascinating. Ever since I was a child, I've wanted to know what others really thought, of me or of other people. Unfortunately there was (and still is) no way to know for sure, unless your name is Edward Cullen, of course. Just think, with the ability to read minds, you'd never have to ask for opinions, you'd be able to tell if someone's lying, and you'd know everyone's thoughts on, well, everything. In competitive situations like games or fights, you'd gain an advantage by knowing your opponent's move before he or she has time to act. The ability is exceptionally potent in situations where the "victim" is unaware of your power to pry into their brain. Mind reading is a useful tool to have because people know to control their mouths but they don't censor their thoughts.

○○○
is Jacob Black better pre-transformation or post-transformation?

Pre-transformation!

Rachel, 15, Georgia

Before Jacob transformed, he was a sweet, innocent little kid with a crush on Bella. Pre-transformation Jacob would never hurt Bella in any way, shape, or form. He liked her but would never pursue his love without her permission. Post-transformation Jacob was rude and blunt and immediately hurt Bella. He pursued his interest in Bella without her permission when he kissed her in *Eclipse*. He meddled in Bella's personal life when he told her she couldn't be bitten by a vampire—bitten, not killed. And later, after his transformation, he became obsessed with imprinting, like in *Breaking Dawn* when he randomly searched a park for a girl to imprint on. In short, Jacob was a much better character pre-transformation. Of course, had Jacob never transformed, the story would be pretty boring after a while. Bella probably would have died after jumping off the cliff because without Jacob's wolf strength he never would have saved her. And that's if she evaded Victoria long enough to jump off the cliff, which she probably wouldn't have without Jacob protecting her.

Post-transformation!

Rachel, 23, Saskatchewan, Canada

Jacob Black is quite a complicated character in the series. Jacob has such a sunny disposition, which is what essentially enables Bella to pull out of her reverie and catatonic state after losing Edward. Pre-transformation Jacob is such a happy-go-lucky kid that he cannot help but bring a smile to Bella's face. Pre-transformation Jacob does not feel angry all the time either, and post-transformation he hates feeling angry, especially around Bella because of the potential to hurt her should he lose control. Pre-transformation, he does not have any responsibility to a legendary duty of his tribe, and he is free to make his own choices regardless of what "the pack leader" wants him to do. Post-transformation, Jacob is enabled to protect Bella from the lurking dangers that haunt her once he transforms, which he never could have done before he became a wolf. He still manages to make Bella smile and feel safe with him, as if there is no void in her life because of Edward, but he cannot betray his pack and unfortunately breaks his promise to never hurt her. Thankfully, his body heat, due to his transformation, allows him to save Bella from freezing, while Edward is unable to help her. There are pros and cons to Jacob transforming, but if Bella had never met Edward, then Jacob pre-transformation would be better for both him and her. Nevertheless, Edward does exist in both their lives, but Jacob's character and personality is still intact post-transformation, and his innately happy disposition makes Jacob Black a great character both pre- and post-transformation. However, I prefer the added bonus of Jacob having the ability to keep a girl warm on those cold winter days.

THE FINAL CALL

When we are first introduced to Jacob Black, he's a sweet 15-year-old kid with a "hint of childish roundness" (*Twilight*, page 119). He's easy to talk to, and Bella becomes instant friends with him. After Edward leaves in *New Moon*, pre-transformation Jacob keeps Bella company. He's the one that makes her laugh again, the one who's there for her when Edward isn't. However, everything changes when Jacob Black transforms into a werewolf. For a long period of time (although it isn't his fault), he can't talk to Bella, and he leaves her in the dark about what's going on. As his love for Bella grows, he employs selfish tactics to make her love him back. When Carlisle calls the Swan residence in *New Moon* (*New Moon*, page 412), Jacob intentionally does not let Bella have the phone even though he knows she wants to talk to Dr. Cullen. Instead, he coldly answers, "He's at the funeral," when asked about Charlie's where-abouts, causing a string of misunderstandings. At the end of *New Moon*, Jacob brings Bella's motorcycles to Charlie's house in order to get her grounded, another act that pre-transformation Jacob would never do. Jake the werewolf also tends to have anger issues, es-pecially when it comes to his love for Bella. He almost loses control at Bella and Edward's wedding when he asks Bella about her honeymoon (*Breaking Dawn*, page 65), and later on he threatens to kill Edward (*Breaking Dawn*, page 67). So, even though post-transformation

Jacob uses his powers to save Bella multiple times, his new adamant and overbearing personality makes me prefer the old, sweet little Jacob.

○○○
should jacob
have imprinted
on renesmee?

Yes!

Rachel, 14, Illinois

I think this question is perhaps one of the most talked-about among *Twilight* fans. Jacob Black is alone, desperate for help, and dealing with utter grief when he imprints on Renesmee. He thinks his best friend is dead, killed by the very enemies he's befriended. He's terrified of what lies ahead of him, describing it as an endless ocean of grief. He's come to the point of murder, wanting to kill anyone and anything he can that has killed the girl he loves. He knows he'll die in the attempt, and he embraces that fact, welcoming it with open arms. When Jacob imprints on Renesmee, it's the stop to all of that. His world changes and he connects with a little brown-eyed baby girl whom he should hate. Think of what would've happened if Jacob hadn't imprinted on Renesmee. Bella's baby, whom she had fought so hard for, would be killed, along with her best friend and possibly some of her family members, all for nothing. Along with that fact, think about Jacob. He would have been miserable! He was left with no one when Bella chose Edward, refusing to be comforted or helped. And where would the story have gone from there? It would have turned into "the miserable life of Jacob Black" while we watch the main character's baby grow up. Why would anyone want to read a story like that?

Savannah, 14, California

Yes! I think it is really cool that they are together. When I started reading the book, I never saw this part coming. I knew that Bella would be with Edward, and but I still really wanted to see more of Jake. He is a really great character, and I would hate for him to just disappear. Considering that Renesmee is a half-vampire/half-human and he is a werewolf, it really gets me thinking about what Jake and Nessie's baby will be like. They are really cute together, too, and their relationship unites the vampires and werewolves. I really want to figure out what happens five or ten years later. It really seems like that Nessie and Jake will be extremely happy together, maybe moving into Bella and Edward's house once they are older. I really love that the imprinting happened, and I don't think the book would have been complete without it.

Dayi, 19, Georgia

Yes, Jacob most definitely should have imprinted on Renesmee. So many people were worried about Jacob's happiness or unhappiness as a result of Bella choosing Edward over him. This is what created Teams Edward and Team Jacob. However, *Breaking Dawn* made both teams unnecessary. Jacob had to have some kind of happy ending. What better way to do that than have him imprint on an extremely crucial character? It was a stroke of genius by Stephenie Meyer to have Jacob imprint on Renesmee. Though it may seem somewhat creepy that he is destined to be with Bella and Edward's daughter since he was in love with Bella and hated Edward, I believe that there could have been no one better for our darling Jacob than the most lovable Nessie. The mistake would have been to leave Jacob still alone and heartbroken, waiting for his one true love. As a result, it beautifully brought the story together and made for one of the best books of the Twilight saga.

Alejandra, 16, California

Before I can answer whether Jacob should have imprinted on Renesmee or not, I would first like to examine the Twilight universe. The Twilight saga is a romance—a very chaste one at that, but a passionate, blood-boiling story nonetheless—in which the two main characters, Bella Swan and Edward Cullen, struggle through the conflicts of their forbidden romance. Everything appears to keep them apart, from a sadistic vampire to a *Rosemary's Baby* vampire-and-human hybrid, but even when the eleventh hour has struck and hope seems nonexistent, their love prevails.

For example, although the transformation from a human into a vampire produces an undeniable blood thirst, Bella magically develops an indifference to it as long as her mind it otherwise occupied. Let us not forget that blood to a newborn vampire is reminiscent of milk to a newborn child; it is a physical factor, not a mental one, and the denial of it triggers a ravenous hunger. And because Bella does not succumb to the animalistic impulse for blood, she is free to spend her time with her child, her husband, and the rest of her family and friends. Does this twist—that Bella does not steadily require what her new body should demand—have a logical explanation? Or does Bella's inexplicable success with vampirism suggest something else?

Twilight is for gratification, something to indulge in for the fairy tale ending. Stephenie Meyer, the author, stated herself that the reasoning behind *Breaking Dawn's* lack of an impressive battle was that it would have resulted in half of the Cullens' demise. Killing off fictional characters was too painful to bear. Twilight sprouted from a vivid dream Stephenie Meyer had one night, which indicates the fantasy a subconscious mind produces. The evidence of an author's self-indulgence cannot be denied after an analysis of Bella Swan's perfect life. The saga takes obvious pleasure in granting Bella everything necessary to obtain the perfect life without any consequences to her past actions. She is not forced to battle a raging blood thirst or sacrifice her relationship with her father or face the Volturi's wrath.

Consequently, in a world of indulgence, of course Jacob Black should have imprinted on Renesmee Cullen. What other reason could have kept him in Bella's life without any romantic tension? Out of Bella's notable six admirers, Jacob Black and Edward Cullen are featured as the most prominent love interests. Bella constantly agonizes over that fact that, although she loves them both, she must decide her future between them. At the end of *Eclipse*, she explains to Jacob that her love for Edward is too powerful to fairly rival her love for him, which is why her love for Jacob could not possibly grow. Causing Jacob pain distresses Bella. She loves him, he is her best friend, and she wants for him to remain present in her life.

Stephenie Meyer has proven that her protagonist is either the luckiest girl alive or she is a self-indulgence. Since the saga gives the appearance of fulfilling its main character's wishes, there is nothing to prevent Bella's wish of always having Jacob in her life. And by having Jacob imprint on her daughter, Renesmee, which causes Jacob's devotion to be focused on one single person, Bella need not worry over any underlying romantic tension between her and Jacob. Her life is truly perfect now.

No!

Elisabeth, 24, Illinois

Pardon the phrasing, but Jacob imprinting on Renesmee was just throwing the dog a bone. We have followed this amazing character throughout the series, and he is in love with Bella. But what happens when this really beloved character in the series isn't going to get the girl? We'll just have him be destined to be with her daughter! Give me a break. It's a bit of a cop-out after everything that we've seen him and Bella go through emotionally with each other. Maybe it was the need for things to be tied up neatly in the end, but I think Stephenie Meyer could have done better than that. I do find it slightly creepy that he knows at her birth that she is the one he is destined to be with. I also hate when Edward calls Jacob "son." He's not your son; in fact, he's been your enemy throughout the entire story. Suddenly everything is all right and wrapped up nice and neat because it's "destiny."

Laura, 16, Middlesbrough, England

I think that Jacob shouldn't have imprinted on Renesmee because, for starters, she's part vampire and he's a werewolf, both of whom are, in Stephenie Meyer's world, sworn mutual enemies. Wouldn't this mean that Jacob should naturally hate Renesmee as he hates vampires in general? Since he is a werewolf, shouldn't this mean he would want to kill her, not love her because of the uncontrollable instinct werewolves have toward vampires? This urge he should feel to kill Renesmee would mean that he couldn't "imprint" on her, because at every turn he should want to rip her apart and burn the pieces. Furthermore, vampires and were-wolves both have a potent sense of smell, and although Renesmee's smell is seen as vampire with traces of human in it, so not so sickly-sweet, Jacob would still not want to be around her because of the vampire smell in her blood. Also, Jacob smells of "wet dog" to vampires, and Renesmee is part vampire, with higher senses than an average human, so Jacob's smell should be disgusting to her.

THE FINAL CALL

I have to admit, Jacob imprinting on Renesmee was a total shocker for me! Now, I do agree when fans say that Renesmee is an unusual and maybe even unrealistic choice for him. She is, after all, a half-vampire, which means that Jacob's natural instinct should be to hate her. But as crazy as it is, I'm glad it happens. For one, the story of Bella, Edward, and their family ends on such a happy note that something would have been off if Jacob had been left in misery. It would've left the fans with a cliffhanger. What would happen to Jacob? Would he find someone to love and be with for the rest of his life? There's a hole in the story when Bella and Edward are officially married and Jacob's pursuit of Bella is over. He needs someone to be with. Second, even though Bella is deeply in love with Edward, she's always torn when it comes to Jacob. She loves him, but only as a dear friend. Bella wishes that Jacob were her brother so he would always be near her. By imprinting on Bella's daughter, Jacob secures his place in Bella's life and, on top of that, Bella will rest assured knowing that her child is in good hands. In conclusion, although the Jacob-Renesmee pair seems a little unrealistic to some fans, it was the best choice Stephenie Meyer could've made for the fate of her characters.

OOO
is there a significance to imprinting, or is it just plain creepy?

It's cool!

Dayi, 19, Georgia

In some ways, imprinting may seem creepy because of our mindset, especially when the object of a werewolf's imprinting is just a toddler or a newborn baby. But if you read the books, you will find out just how non-creepy it can be. Imprinting is significant simply because when you imprint, you find your true love. You find the one person you are supposed to be with forever. In the world of Twilight, however, they speculate why the imprinting happens. Its significance may lie in continuing the werewolf's bloodline, therefore ensuring that the shape-shifting gene carries on. Whatever the reason for imprinting, I believe it is significant to the story and those that it happens to. In truth, I wish that we all imprinted. It would make finding our soul mate and being happy a heck of a lot easier. Plus, it would probably make men in general less wayward in their affections toward the ones they are supposed to love.

Shannon, 29, South Carolina

Stephenie must have had the idea that Jacob imprints on Bella's daughter from the beginning, since it somehow just seems to fall in place. Though, yes, it is very creepy, since the wolves are imprinting on small children, it is also kind of heartwarming to know that Jacob will eventually be with someone that he loves just as much as Bella loves Edward. I think it signifies Bella and Jacob's bond that they have had since *New Moon*. They will always be family, and they will be able to remain friends.

Rachel, 15, Georgia

Stephenie Meyer walked a fine line when she wrote of imprinting. On the one hand, imprinting could be viewed as stalker-ish, dangerous, and in some cases, like pedophilia. Stephenie Meyer manages to write about imprinting so it doesn't have to be romantic; the imprinter just wants what's best for the imprintee. The reader knows from the details given that if Emily, Rachel or Renesmee fell in love with someone who wasn't their imprinter and told their imprinters to never see them again, Sam, Paul, and Jacob would walk away without a second glance. Of course, their hearts would be broken forever, but they would never let their imprintees see that because they love them too much. If Stephenie Meyer were to sway either way on imprinting and make it so the imprinter could never be without the imprintee, or make it so it was immediately romantic, imprinting would become gross and stalker-ish and the readers would be turned off by it immediately. As long as Stephenie Meyer can walk that fine line she has made for herself, imprinting is significant, romantic, sweet, and completely appropriate.

It's creepy!

Alejandra, 16, California

Imprinting is the term used to describe a shape-shifter's permanent attachment to a perfectly matched companion. We, as readers, first witness the relationship between a shape-shifter and his imprint in *New Moon* with Sam Uley and Emily Young. The blatant adoration is so difficult to resist that, although Sam had been dating Emily's cousin, Leah Clearwater, at the time, Emily could not resist returning his affections. Imprinting is not something that influences a shape-shifter's feelings toward someone, but it is a force so powerful it cannot be withheld.

Much like Romeo and Juliet's love at first sight, a shape-shifter knows his ideal "mate" by simply laying eyes on her without having any previous knowledge of his prospective mate's history, personality, or current life. There is no recognized science or logic behind a shape-shifter's inexplicable knowledge of who his soul mate is, which leaves one to question whether this "imprinting" is true love or animal attraction. Is this meant to be romantic or plain creepy? I, personally, find this idea extremely disturbing and insulting. If I were Emily, I could be offended by the fact that someone doesn't have to know my likes, beliefs, and habits before deciding that he is madly in love with me. It would be as though there is nothing worth understanding, like I'm a cardboard cutout of a fantasy.

Imprinting is not only a strange concept for the shape-shifter but also for the imprintee. "Love at first sight" happens through sight, obviously, which first involves examining each other's physical appearance to discover the potential for love. This alone is superficial, but what contributes to the shallowness is accepting this method as an excuse for falling in love. Why would someone allow themselves to be claimed by sight rather than soul? A soul cannot be viewed, cannot be captured on film or reflected in the mirror, but a face can. Which would you rather have treasured?

According to Sam Uley's theory, imprinting is a mechanism with a Darwinian twist; shape-shifters find their ideal "mate" to produce the strongest offspring possible. This is "survival of the fittest." So, taking Sam's theory into account, this "love at first sight" is more animal attraction than affection. After all, in the animal kingdom, it is quite normal for an alpha to have the ability to choose whatever female he wants because nature predicts that with her, his offspring will be far superior to others'.

Because imprinting happens so swiftly and so unexpectedly, no actual romance takes place. There are no frenzied butterflies at the accidental touch of hands, no racing hearts at the utterance of "I love you" for the first time, and no credible reasons behind the "love." Imprinting has no other significance but to match a shape-shifter with someone compatible by nature and not necessarily by personality, considering the lack of personal contact required for this method of falling in love. Its importance, based on Sam Uley's theory, concentrates on genetic improvement because "love at first sight" has nothing to do with character.

THE FINAL CALL

Imprinting has always been an interesting concept to me. How can a werewolf lay eyes on someone and be so absolutely sure it's his soul mate? And what if the imprintee doesn't reciprocate the feelings? Take the situation of Quil and Claire, for example. Jacob is so sure that when Claire grows up she will choose Quil as her mate (*Eclipse*, page 176), it's almost as if she's in a binding contract. Her fate has already been decided for her, and she has no say in it whatsoever. And what about Paul and Rachel? Neither Billy nor Jacob is thrilled about Paul imprinting on their family member, and it leaves them in a sticky situation because there's nothing they can do about it (*Breaking Dawn*, page 148). Since not every werewolf is guaranteed to imprint, the wolves have to live every day wondering if they're going to find their soul mate or if they should just settle for a "normal" relationship. Of course, we all know that there *is* significance to imprinting. As Alejandra said, the werewolves need a way to produce the strongest offspring possible. But with imprinting comes consequences. Sam breaks Leah's heart because when he see her cousin, Emily, he immediately falls in love with her. So while there is a significance to imprinting (and in some situations it *can* be a tad bit creepy), I personally find it terribly inconvenient.

○○○
is bella's transition from phoenix to forks too unrealistic?

Yes, it's unrealistic!

Rachel, 15, Georgia

Yes, it's very unrealistic. When Bella moves from Phoenix to Forks, she literally cuts her Phoenix life away from her. She has no friends she keeps in contact with in Phoenix, and in fact she mentions absolutely nobody that she knows in Phoenix other than her mom and Phil. Bella lived in Phoenix for 12 of her 17 years, and at least someone there had to notice she was gone and e-mail her. Bella could have at least thought, "Oh

I miss that girl who used to be on the basketball team. She was really sweet." Bella has literally no emotional baggage when she comes to Forks, which is extremely unrealistic to begin with.

No, it's believable!

Shannon, 29, South Carolina

It's not unrealistic, just different. We think that people who are content with where they are and what they are doing would want to stay that way. But we learn that Bella is so selfless that she just wants the people she loves to be happy. The thing that makes her transition so believable is the fact that she falls irrevocably in love with Edward. Sometimes when you love someone, you don't see beyond that. The bad things just seem to disappear, or are worth enduring, and you focus on the good. Bella discovers a world that no other human really knows. It's interesting and new. It's living on the edge, an adrenaline rush.

Shelley, 29, California

Bella's adjustment to Forks after living in Phoenix was an excellent portrayal of climate shock. Is it too unrealistic? I think not. People who thrive in the sun seem to have biological connections to its presence. Fill the sky with clouds and produce rain of any kind and it seems the end of the world has arrived. All of a sudden people are wearing galoshes and parkas and begging for the return of that big yellow ball in the sky. For Bella it was worse. She didn't just move to a location known for having a rainy "season." As Edward said, she moved to the wettest place in the continental United States. Over the course of several hours, her world turned from blue, sun-filled skies to misty and gray with a side of cold and wet.

Think about it. If you live in California, Phoenix, or any other "sunny" location, you might fall asleep at to random noise consisting of crickets, traffic, and the occasional breeze. Eventually you become attuned to your surroundings, and it all melts into silence. Bella moved to an environment where creaking branches, crackling ice, and the constant drumming of rain filled her background. Sensory overload anyone? It makes perfect sense that her first days in Forks were miserable. She couldn't sleep. She wasn't yet desensitized to the ambient sounds of her new world. Exhaustion only adds weight to the gloomy sky when you aren't friends with it. While most people have a love-hate relationship with the weather (they complain when it's cold and beg for summer, only to quickly tire of the heat and wish for winter), Bella had a hate-hate relationship with the weather of Forks. Not only did she dislike the fact that the dismal atmosphere was holding captive her beloved sun, she scorned the many new hazards this place introduced her to. Her clumsiness was a minor inconvenience before. Now it was being given the tools to cause her bodily harm. She needed time to acclimate to her surroundings. Most of all, she needed a distraction. Adjustment is always easiest when it occurs in the background of our circumstance. When she met Edward, the weather didn't seem quite as unbearable as it once had. Her frame of reference changed. The skies of Forks eventually stopped being her enemy ... and became the skies that protected the one she loved. A perfectly realistic transition.

THE FINAL CALL

In the beginning of *Twilight*, Bella comments on how much she loved Phoenix (*Twilight*, page 4) and yet, after that, she never mentions anything about it. No memories, no friends, no flashbacks. Surely she had *some* friends in the "vigorous, sprawling city." Even if she "didn't relate well to people [her] age" (*Twilight*, page 10), she lived there for 12 years of her life! For these reasons, Bella's move from Phoenix to Forks seemed a little unrealistic to me at first. But as I read on,

I realized that there was a good, solid reason for why she seemed to forget her previous life: Edward Cullen. Bella first sees Edward in the very beginning of *Twilight* (*Twilight*, page 18) and from that moment on she's either too busy being entranced by his aloofness or too busy being in love with him to care about anything else. As Shannon so accurately stated, "sometimes when you love someone, you don't see beyond that." In Forks, Bella is thrust into a world of vampires, a world that she never thought could have existed, a world that completely overshadows her "normal" life back in Arizona. This great shock factor would have definitely contributed to her seeming lack of concern for Phoenix. In addition, Bella's willingness to put Phoenix behind and focus on Forks parallels her fearless decision later in the series to give up her human life and become a vampire. Bella's transition from Phoenix to Forks isn't really unrealistic; as Shannon said, it's just different.

○○○

would Bella have been better off in phoenix or in forks?

Forks

Elisabeth, 24, Illinois

Bella would have been safer, theoretically anyway, in Phoenix with her mother than in Forks. However, if Bella had not gone to Forks, she would not have met Edward and set into motion the events that would change the rest of her life. She may have been "better off" in a sense in Phoenix, but she also would have been a boring, miserable teenage girl, but happy that her mom was happy. She would not have had the life that, in the end, she sees as her destiny and fate. And of course, we would not have had the story to follow. She needed that drama and emotional despair to be interesting to those of us who are reading her story. Without it, she would have just been a boring, unhappy teenage girl. By coming to Forks, she became "the new girl," the one girl that Edward finally showed interest in, a girl that hung out with vampires and wolves and had two men vying for her attention and her heart. All of that tied together makes her far more interesting and worth actually paying attention to than if she had stayed in Phoenix.

Deidre, 22, Alberta, Canada

We wouldn't have had a story if Bella had stayed in Phoenix. Things happen the way they are supposed to happen, in life or in a story. Bella's life in Forks may not have been the one she chose for herself before meeting Edward, but that is how things work out. She found the love of her life and had a child. Her life never was and never will be perfect, but she found essentially what everyone is looking for and that is love. She found love in so many forms and is so lucky to have so many wonderful and caring people in her life.

Dayi, 19, Georgia

Despite the trouble that befell Bella in Forks, she was much better off there. Even though she suffers vampire attacks, lots of guilt, and heartache, she still would have been more miserable without little ol' Forks. There she meets her future family, gets to know her loving father, makes the best of friends, and finds the one she is destined to be with—not necessarily in that order. Bella definitely does not regret her move, so why should anyone else?

THE FINAL CALL

As expected, Twilighters called Forks the better place for Bella. True, Bella would have technically been better off (not to mention way safer) had she stayed in Phoenix. She would have led a normal life, probably with a normal, *human* boyfriend. But what's the fun of living the life of an average teenage girl? Why not add a vampire boyfriend into the mix? In Forks, Bella has the opportunity to experience a whole new world filled with vampires and werewolves. She develops powerful relationships and surrounds herself with people who are willing to love her forever (literally). Bella's able to obtain something intrinsically rare—a relationship with a vampire boyfriend. Even though Bella has to overcome many obstacles in Forks, namely being attacked by rogue vampires, hiding secrets from her friends and family, and giving birth to a half-vampire baby, in the end, the fact that she finds the love of her life makes Forks the right choice.

○○○
is charlie swan a good dad?

Yes!

Deidre, 22, Alberta, Canada

Charlie is a good dad. He didn't have a lot of time to spend with Bella while she was growing up, but he does the best job he could when she moves in with him. I believe it is never easy to be a parent, but to be a single dad to a teenage daughter whom you haven't really helped raise isn't an easy thing. He only wants his daughter to be happy, as any parent does, and he allows her to grow and change to become the person she wants to be. He isn't afraid to punish her either, which is what a good parent should do. He is her parent first and her friend second, exactly how it should be.

Rachel, 15, Georgia
Charlie Swan had fatherhood pushed upon him rather quickly. Of course, he was a father for 17 years, but he never really spent any time with his daughter. He expected her to be a normal teenager and try to sneak out, and he tried to prevent her from sneaking out. How on earth was he supposed to know her boyfriend snuck into her bedroom every night? Although occasionally he may seem naive, what evidence did he have to suspect Bella of anything? If she had been sneaking out to see Edward and he didn't realize it, then he would be a clueless dad, but under the circumstances, he does the best he can.

Sort of...

Alex, 17, London, England
I don't feel he's an especially brilliant father, but neither do I think he's a bad father. He comes across as slightly lazy around the house, but he makes up for it with all he has to handle being police chief. Generally speaking, he appears to respect Bella's privacy and is fairly relaxed with her, though at the same time he is not afraid to ground her when he feels it's necessary. Throughout

the series, it's also made apparent just how much he cares for his daughter and her well-being, such as his caring manner toward her when Edward leaves and his protection over her when Edward comes back. It is clear he doesn't want to see her hurt again. Finally, he forgives her whenever she runs off or leaves him in the dark about something.

THE FINAL CALL

The majority of fans seem to agree that Charlie Swan is a pretty decent dad. Of course, living alone for most of his life didn't prepare him well for life with Bella, but Charlie is willing to adjust for his daughter. When Bella announced that she wanted to move to Forks, police chief Swan was no doubt surprised. However, he quickly makes her feel at home and even surprises her with a car (*Twilight*, page 7). Throughout the series, Charlie constantly tries to help Bella and make her feel at home, even though at times his reticent nature betrays the fact that he really does care for his daughter. Charlie wants what every good parent wants for their child—the best they can get. He is always very protective of Bella, setting curfews and rules for her when needed (*Twilight*, page 483) and punishing those who hurt his daughter (*New Moon*, page 549). Given the circumstances—try raising a teenage daughter with a vampire boyfriend—Charlie Swan gives his best when it comes to being a father.

OOO

what is one major downfall of the series?

Bella's personality

Elisabeth, 24, Illinois

My biggest issue with the series is that occasionally Bella is extremely whiney. As I sat reading *New Moon*, I wanted to feel sympathy for her, and I did at first, but eventually I just wanted to tell her to get over it. I understand the concept of soul mates and tried to look it from the perspective that half of her was missing, which honestly was the only thing that got me through *New Moon*. I wanted to shake her, and say, "Get over it and look at the amazing guy that is there in your life.

Yeah, Jacob, remember him? The guy you used to feel better and in the end fell for? He is standing in front of you with open arms and a heart that already has you in it, and all you can think about is how alone you are because Edward left you." My other issue with the series is that at times it is a bit anticlimactic. We never do get a good fight, even though several are set up throughout the books. It is also a little predictable. We know Bella is going to end up with Edward because they are soul mates, and this is young adult writing, so we have to be happy and positive in the end. As a reader, I know everyone is going to be happy and paired up and everything will tied up nice and neat with a little bow for me.

The obsessive fans

Nicole, 21, Pennsylvania

My answer to this will probably anger most fans of the Twilight saga, simply because my answer is exactly them: the fans. Nothing has been worse for Twilight than its fans (not even the awful, awful way the movies have turned out). It's a harsh claim, but it must be said. Stay with me, and I will explain.

Twilight fans are positively rabid. It's no secret. They are obsessive to the point of literally weeping over minute-long teaser trailers for the films (one need only read comments on BellaAndEdward.com to know this is true).

It is the fans that have both made the saga a smashing success and at the same time completely ruined Twilight for outsiders. I know many people who refuse to give the series a chance simply because they cannot stand the insanity of the fans—one of my friends has a younger sister who for months upon months would not shut up about Twilight, and thus my friend is completely disgusted by all things related to the saga. Twilighters fiercely declare themselves "Cullenists" or "Team Edward/Jacob" loyalists, all to the severe annoyance of outsiders. Few things are more obnoxious than being around a Twi-hard who can't stop chattering about their desperate love for Edward Cullen or how Jacob is better than Edward or what their favorite lines are from the books. We fans love to talk about that stuff, but to everyone else, it is insufferable.

A huge percentage of Twilight's fan base seems to be made up of girls from the ages of, say, 13 to 17 (no citation available, this is my own observation). This means that Twilight falls right into that age where girls voraciously cling to things—they don't just like things, they obsess over them. And by "obsess," I mean this stuff is life and death to girls. We all know that phase, we all have been there. We've all found that actor or fandom that we had to buy every poster of and talk to everyone about, or names and images we doodled on our notebooks, shows we cried over if we missed a single episode, or whatever.

For me, it was The Lord of the Rings and actor Orlando Bloom. I was completely obsessed—*painfully* obsessed, and everyone around me knew I was that girl who loved those movies. It's something most, if not all, girls go through and will get over.

However, the fact that this group of fans will someday reach an age where they can talk about something other than Edward Cullen doesn't do the Twilight saga's dignity any good. Instead of calm, dignified, and reasonable fans, Twilight's fan base consists mostly of screaming preteen girls who will gouge your eyes out if you so much as suggest that Edward is a lame vampire or that Twilight may not be the best piece of literature in the history of the written word (which—brace yourselves, fans—it isn't).

Now, I don't mean to insult fans of this series. I am a fan. I'm a big fan. I *love* the books. And I was a "preteen" too once, so I'm not blaming them for being what they are. I finally resigned to read the series after the first three had already been published (about 2.8 seconds before the series' popularity completely exploded into the phenomenon it is now) and I absolutely flew through them. I knew it wasn't the greatest book series ever written. The writing can't even compare to other things I've read (i.e., yes, fellow Twilighters, I'm going to say it: *Harry Potter*). But I was completely in love with the characters, and it was easy and satisfying to read. I couldn't get enough of Edward and Bella's sappy love for one another, of whimsical Alice and Jasper, of the inner workings of the wolf pack, of the wicked Volturi…. It was thoroughly enjoyable. When *Breaking Dawn* was released, my friend and I went to the beach and read it like fiends. We annoyed the rest of our friends a little, but it became a joke.

The level of obsession that surrounds this series has sparked immeasurable backlash. Just take a stroll through Cheezburger.com's section on celebrities and pop culture and you will find countless captioned pictures insulting the Twilight saga. One, showing a group of "Twilight moms" who are all holding *Twilight* posters excitedly, it is captioned as "Grounds for divorce." There's no denying that Twilight has become a joke—it's hard to watch TV or surf the Internet without noting a crack at Twilight or someone insulting the quality of Stephenie Meyer's writing. A lot of this teasing is unfair. Fans know that Stephenie Meyer's vampires don't "sparkle" the way nonreaders think (or the way the crappy effect in the movie illustrates); light simply refracts off of their skin differently. And her vampires aren't wimpy—critics obviously have no knowledge of the vicious "newborns" in Meyer's novels. But the fact that fans have so avidly drawn attention to the series by being *so obsessive* has inevitably inspired people to make fun of it. Admitting to enjoyment of Twilight is met with groans and rolling eyes. The backlash the fans have created has even made me feel sheepish about liking the series. A friend of mine has expressed the same sentiments, and I'm sure others would agree with us. (Someone is undoubtedly going to boast that I'm "not a true fan" if I consider Twilight a guilty pleasure. To this person, I roll my eyes in your general direction.)

This is truly a shame, because the Twilight saga *is* an enjoyable series. The books are good, easy reads with addicting characters. We live vicariously through these books because, let's face it, we all not-so-secretly want to be romanced by a vampire. The books give us exactly what we want—and I don't call it a weakness. It's just a satisfying read, something that is extremely fun to get into. No, it's no Harry Potter (to compare the two is truly unfair for more than one reason, but that's another issue entirely) but so what? It is what it is, and fans should love it *for what it is* instead of trying to shove Twilight down the throat of every non-Twilight-reading heathen. To say that Twilighters have ruined Twilight isn't to say that they have ruined the success of the series—the books and films have raked in amounts of money that are truly ridiculous. But they certainly have branded Twilight with a horrible, horrible stigma that outsiders simply are unable to break through—and I don't blame them. I fear that *Twilight* won't be remembered as an enchanting teenage-romance novel, but as "that horrible fad that annoyed the s––– out of us all." And anyone who angrily attacks me—or this article—is only supporting my point. Go on and love Twilight, my friends, but please don't smother all that's good about it.

The plotline of the series

Alejandra, 16, California

Getting published doesn't exactly require literary skills or experience, which is why pedestrian writing is easily forgivable and often overlooked. The strength in a novel is established in the development of characters and the intrigue of a plot; if a story keeps a reader engaged, a misplaced comma or a misused word will not detract anything from the actual story. Taking this into account, the Twilight saga's one major downfall is the lack of a compelling plotline.

Readers may say whatever they like in response to a novel's weak character development or average writing, but the core of any fantasy novel should be its plot. For example, I have a friend who is currently reading the House of Night series, and despite her distaste for the protagonist's cringe-worthy dialogue and ridiculous number of boyfriends, my friend's attention is caught by the creative story line. The strange need to discover what happens next is enough to convince a reader to continue with even the most juvenile of series.

While *Twilight* offers a sparkly alternative to traditional vampires, it does not delve into the components of vampire integration in the human world and instead focuses on the main character's relationship with her boyfriend, Edward Cullen. The mystery in *Twilight* is ruined by the book's back story, which indicates that Edward is a vampire, so the first 300 pages consist of Bella's torment over Edward's puzzling behavior her discovering of the secret readers already know. *Twilight* does not have a semblance of a valid plot until its last 100 pages, and even then the plot feels contrived and the villain's motive is weak.

New Moon offers little besides a girl's depression resulting from breaking up with her boyfriend, and even that is skimmed over by using four pages titled with months. Yes, Jacob Black's shape-shifter transformation is involved, but that hardly merits being called a plot, considering how once the discovery is made, the story does not progress into anything memorable. Only at the end do readers reach the beginning of a plot—the Volturi. Edward, devastated by the supposed death of Bella Swan, plans to publicize the vampire secret so the Volturi will end his life. The Volturi's duty is to conceal their immortal secret and punish those with other intentions, and because Bella is a mortal aware of vampires, the Cullens have broken the Volturi's single rule. The climax of *New Moon* fizzles out because Bella and the Cullens do not receive a punishment; the only consequence is the Volturi's looming expectation of Bella's vampirism.

Eclipse concentrates on Bella's decision between Jacob and Edward more than it focuses on Seattle's recent newborn attacks and their connection to Bella. Once Bella realizes that Victoria is recruiting a newborn army with the sole purpose of her death, the story picks up the pace and suggests an exciting battle with dozens of bloodthirsty vampires. This leaves readers in suspense, expecting action, except that when Eclipse reaches its climax, a brief Edward-and-Victoria encounter substitutes for the actual newborn battle. Its intended plot occurs outside of the text.

Unlike the three novels that precede it, *Breaking Dawn* actually completes a plotline that readers are able to experience from start to finish. Bella's dangerous pregnancy not only endangers her own life but also divides the shape-shifter pack in two, with Sam and Jacob both as alphas to separate packs. Bella's pregnancy reaches its climax with a graphic birth scene where Edward rips open her stomach with his teeth, which leads to Bella's emergency transformation. After Bella transitions into vampirism, *Breaking Dawn* continues with a narrative similar to a diary filled with accounts of a typical day, until a member of the Denali clan, Irina, witnesses Bella's daughter's astonishing vampire traits, which are reminiscent of vampire history's illegal immortal children. The previous plotline reemerges as a catalyst to accelerate the Volturi's dreaded visit to Forks, Washington; and at their arrival, like in Eclipse, readers are left anticipating a massive battle between all the Volturi and a handful of vampire covens. But after a lengthy conversation and one casualty, there is no battle; the Volturi leave, shame-faced, and the Cullens, along with their vampire clan allies, are free to live their lives in peace. Despite the fact that *Breaking Dawn*'s first plot is fully realized, the third portion of the novel provides readers with an avoidance of conflict.

The Twilight saga's major downfall is its lack of a concrete plot. Whenever a plotline grows interesting, furthering the story, it diminishes before an actual climax can be reached. Though romance is a prominent area in the saga, the introduction of other story lines eliminates the chance of Bella and Edward's forbidden romance being the only plotline. And their romance is repetitive and dragged out, so even if it were the saga's solitary plot, the series would also be lacking in the story department. Either way, the Twilight saga misses a plot; all the details are there, ready to be molded, but instead of creating an original and unexpected story, the series favors easily avoided predicaments.

THE FINAL CALL

All three fans here gave interesting responses. I agree with Elisabeth when she says that Bella often comes across as whiney; like Nicole, I have seen and experienced firsthand the obsessive and "rabid" actions of Twi-hards; and I understand where Alejandra is coming from when she complains about the predictable plotline. But for me, the single most annoying thing about the Twilight saga is the fact that it is so easily made fun of. I don't know about you, but every time I try to explain to a non-Twilighter what the series is about, their reaction is always something along the lines of "Wow, that sounds awfully cheesy!" And I don't blame them, because you just can't do the Twilight saga justice in a couple of sentences; it almost always comes off as either blatantly cheesy or just completely ridiculous. I get weird looks from people all the time, and it's really hard to convince someone to read a book they are already skeptical about. The media coverage on the series doesn't really help the situation either (but of course, that's not anyone's fault). The media's attempts to briefly summarize the saga give critics (who probably have never actually opened a copy of *Twilight*) something to laugh about and make fun of. A human girl falling in love with a vampire! Critics have a field day with that one! It's just so sad to see such a great series being portrayed in an inaccurately negative light.

⭕⭕⭕
what is the best thing about the twilight saga?

Dayi, 19, Georgia

The love and continuity of the story is the best thing about the Twilight saga. Bella was not fickle at all, despite the fact that she fell in love with Jacob as well as Edward. In all honesty, who could resist Jacob's charm when he chose to unleash it full force? But Bella fell into some hard-core love with Edward. When he left her, she went into such a decline that cynics took lightly but other readers could relate to. When you lose a love like that, you do not easily get over it and move on. Stephenie Meyer did not let Bella do that, and it was a good call. Bella is one of those people that choose to love with all their hearts, no holding back, and you just don't see that often anymore. She remained faithful to Edward, not out of obligation, but because she adored him so much and saw her future with him. There is no easy way to let go of the life one has embraced as fully as Bella did with her life as a vampire. In the end, her constancy paid off and she got the life she wanted and more. The love shared by all the characters in the books and the persistence of Bella and Edward's affection toward each other make for the best things in the Twilight saga.

Deidre, 22, Alberta, Canada

The best thing about the series is that it encourages people to read and explore another world. It helps open up their minds and can inspire people to realize that there is hope and love out there in the world. If a human girl and a vampire can find love, there is hope for everyone.

THE FINAL CALL

The best thing about the Twilight saga for me has always been the massive fan base and the connection that all of the fans have with each other. As crazy and obsessive some Twi-hards seem to be, they are always there to support and help each other out when needed. I've made great friends because of Twilight, and I know of people who have become best friends because of the books. Twilighters have the opportunity to meet other fans who are just as crazy about the series as they are at conventions, premieres, and other gatherings, and it's truly great to see them bond over a common interest. It's almost as if, when you're with other Twi-hards, nothing matters but Twilight. In addition, wherever a Twilight cast or crew member is in need of something, the fans help out! I'm sure you all remember the Michael Welch sock mission hosted by the Twilight Lexicon, or Peter Facinelli's mission to get 1,000,000 Twitter followers in exchange for a Rob DeFranco bikini dance. In both situations, the fans jumped in and offered their assistance to help reach the goal. The Twilight saga has the power to join people together and inspire great causes, creating a very unique fan base.

○○○
should Bella have ended up with Edward or Jacob?

Edward

Rachel, 23, Saskatchewan, Canada

As much as I came to appreciate and love Jacob for who he is and how great I believe him to be with Bella, I know that Bella and Edward are meant to be together. Most people are probably in "Camp Edward" with a spare few who are in "Camp Jacob"; however, Edward is the ultimate partner for Bella. Edward has his faults, such as being overly possessive, controlling, and worrisome of others' potential for harm where Bella is concerned, but his heart is in the right place. Edward's actions are motivated by Bella's safety, even from himself, and he truly loves her to the very end. Edward proves that what Bella wants is more important than what he wants, and he shows us that toward the end of *New Moon* and during the tent scene in *Eclipse* when he is willing to give her up to Jacob if he is the one she wants in her life. Jacob is without a doubt a good match for Bella as well, but unfortunately he would always be her second choice no matter her feelings for him. The story would have felt different had she chosen Jacob. Bella and Jacob are cute and intriguing together, and even though I think they have a great chemistry, I do not believe the series would have done as well if she had chosen Jacob over Edward. In most stories, people do not want to read how the girl ends up not with the guy who was "written for her" but with the best friend—it would always appear to be a consolation ending to the story no matter how great the consolation guy. Even though some may secretly still wish Jacob had won Bella's heart in the end, and part of me wishes that I could read that version of the story, Edward is the one for Bella. No matter how much I love Jacob and how painful I believe that decision to have been for Bella, I know that she made the right choice to move forward and be with Edward.

Rachel, 14, Illinois

This is the question most debated around the world among the Twilight saga fans, is it not? There are some of the most opinionated minds in the world of Twilight debating their ideas with each other even as I write this now. Before I go any further with my answer though, I want to make my opinion clear: Bella should have, under any and all circumstances, ended up with Edward in the end. Now please Team Jacob fans, don't give up on me yet! The first and foremost reason Bella should have ended up with Edward is the most obvious one: Stephenie Meyer wrote it that way. It's her story after all, and therefore what did happen, should have happened. The second reason is that Bella is in love with Edward, and Edward is in love with Bella. Here it comes. I can just hear the Team Jacob fans screaming, "But Jacob loved Bella and Bella loved Jacob too!" I believe that at one point in *Eclipse*, there is a clear distinction between Bella's two loves. She loves Jacob, and she is in love with Edward. There is a big difference between the two, which Stephenie Meyer writes about Bella distinguishing. Though there are many points and reasons why Bella should've ended up with Edward, these are the main two.

Elizabeth, 16, California

Despite the fact that I am Team Jacob, I think Bella did the right thing when she picked Edward. Jacob did not imprint on Bella, so he would have left her and gone with whoever it was that he did imprint on. Bella would have ended up abandoned just like Leah, and Jacob would have had no control over it. Remember what Edward told Jacob in the clearing in *Eclipse*: He would watch over Bella and wait for the time when Jacob had imprinted so they could be together. Either way, Bella and Edward would be together in the end.

Dayi, 19, Georgia

Bella most definitely should have ended up with Edward. If she had stayed with Jacob, it would have resulted in unhappiness all around. Jacob would never have been with the girl he was supposed to imprint on, Bella would only have lived with a half love, and Edward would have ended up alone when he deserved to be with the person he cared for. The story is perfect as is because Jacob gets his true, fated love and Edward and Bella end up together as they were destined to. Stephenie Meyer's ending is undoubtedly the best resolution.

THE FINAL CALL

We've all heard the Team Edward/Team Jacob debates hosted by Twilighters around the world. Because there are usually a good number of people on Jacob's side, I was surprised to hear from all the fans that Edward was the right choice for Bella. Of course, I'm not challenging that thought; I always believed that Bella should have ended up with Edward. For one, it's what Bella wanted early on. From the end of *Twilight* on, Bella is dead set on becoming a vampire and living the rest of eternity with Edward (*Twilight*, page 474). Jacob is always her best friend, and even though she loves him dearly, she is *in love* with Edward (thank you, Rachel).

Second, Jacob and Bella's relationship would not have lasted long due to the fact that Jacob would eventually imprint. Jacob states in *Eclipse* that he has not found his soul mate yet (*Eclipse*, page 124), which clearly indicates that Bella is not meant for him. Sure, he thinks he's in love with Bella, but that's before he finds his "mystical, wolfy connection" with his imprintee. Things would have ended badly with him and Bella, resulting in heartbreak and agony for not only them, but for Edward as well. As Elizabeth pointed out, Jacob and Bella's story would have been very similar to that of Leah and Sam (*Eclipse*, page 123). Above all,

Edward is willing to do whatever it takes to satisfy and/or save Bella. His departure in *New Moon,* as painful as it is for both him and Bella, is to protect the love of his life. Bella and Edward are meant to be together, and I'm grateful for how the saga ends.

○○○
would the series be as intriguing if bella picked jacob over edward?

Yes!

Alison (LostinBelieving), 14, New Jersey

My answer is yes. Because of Bella's never-ending problems with other vampires, the series probably would still have been intriguing. The Volturi would be back, or Edward's story would still need some telling. The thing is, if Bella had chosen Jacob over Edward, there would have to have been a big enough reason for her choosing him. Like if she never went to save Edward, or if her love for Jacob were bigger than her love for Edward.

Either way, the reason would have to be so insane that it changed the whole series and its outcome.

If Jacob were her choice, the fans would still want to know what happened to Edward. Do you honestly think he would just leave Bella after loving her so deeply? Of course he would, but he might keep tabs on her through Alice or something. Either way, he would turn out heartbroken. And admit it, most books don't end that way. Edward is too big a character, no matter if you love or hate him. His story would need to be told after being rejected by his true love.

And many of Bella's problems would still go unsolved if she picked Jacob. Like Victoria. Let's say that Bella had chosen Jacob at the end of Eclipse. Would Edward have still killed Victoria? Probably, but the Volturi would still be after her, since she would never have changed. Either way, Edward had brought Victoria too much into his world for her to just escape all of it. I honestly don't think that the werewolves would win against the Volturi, no matter how many of them there were. They would need some help from the Cullens, but they would probably be long gone by then.

Not only that, but Stephenie Meyer might need to go and talk about Jacob and Bella's relationship after she chooses him. So Jacob's happy, but what about

Bella? Would it be possible that she could have second thoughts about her choice? In Breaking Dawn, there wasn't a chance of her changing her mind about Edward since she was changed into a vampire. But if she chose Jacob, her actions could lead her to thoughts of whether or not she chose the right person.

There would also be the fact of Jacob imprinting. In the series, he imprints on Renesmee. But if Jacob ended up with Bella, throughout the series the characters would still have that inside worry that if he imprinted on someone else, that would leave Bella by herself. Like Edward, she would end up depressed.

So if you think about it, there are infinite twists and turns that could have happened in the story. Even if Bella ended up with Jacob, Stephenie Meyer would have found a way to make the series just as amazing with things she had already planted into the saga.

No!

Hannah, 16, England, UK

This is one of those questions that can cause strong opinions to be spoken aloud among the Twilight fans. If we think about it carefully, Jacob is still technically a child throughout most of the saga. Yes, in *Breaking Dawn* he appears more adult, but his old habits die hard. Jacob is rather immature, impatient, and a constant grump if he doesn't get his own way. Don't get me wrong, Jacob is the type of boy/man I could see myself falling in love with, but the only reason I could is because people like Edward Cullen do not exist in the real world. People like Jacob do (forgetting that he's a werewolf).

In my personal opinion, if Bella picked Jacob, there wouldn't be a story to tell. With Jacob I feel no risk, no danger, and no pure passion. Jacob is safe, a person whom the majority of people could count as a good friend. If Bella were to choose him over Edward, I can guarantee a lot of fans would have closed the book and said, "Edward subjects himself to unbearable pain every day, just because he loves you. Then you go and pick Jacob!" (Not a pretty thought.) I think it would be impossible to meet someone like Edward then choose to spend your life with another person. Edward has that effect on people (ha ha).

So my opinion is no, the series would not be as intriguing if Bella decided to give her heart away to Jacob. Edward is a strong character—the more dominant character. He has a huge part to play, and the most unique to say the least. He needs Bella, and Bella needs him. I don't personally think Jacob needs Bella. If she were to die, do you really think Jacob would seek out suicide due to his heartbreak and unbearable depression? I think not. Time will heal Jacob, but it would not heal Edward.

I can see the other opinions of this, though, and they do prove a good point. Maybe if Bella had chosen Jacob the story would have taken a completely different turn. A happy life, children, family, and the normalcy of everyday things. But remember, Bella doesn't feel normal, and I think she needs Edward to match her soul.

Elisabeth, 24, Illinois

It would not have been as intriguing if Bella picked Jacob instead of Edward. Jacob is the logical choice for Bella. He is safe and secure, and her father already knows him and his family. Jacob is the more socially acceptable choice. So he would be a much more boring choice for us to read about. With Edward, Bella is alienated from her friends at school as well as from Jacob and his friends. She has hard choices to make and eventually has to decide whether giving up everything that she knows and cares about in her life at that moment is worth it to be with Edward forever. Without the drama and emotional despair, the story would not be nearly as intriguing. Jacob is the logical choice, but Edward is the far more interesting one.

THE FINAL CALL

If Bella backed out at the last minute and decided to live the rest of her life with Jacob, the series would be equally intriguing to me. Now, "intriguing" doesn't necessarily mean "enjoyable," as I would much rather have Bella end up with Edward (contrary to the title of this book), but let's pretend for a moment. Many fans say that Bella's life with Jacob would be less exciting because, as Elisabeth pointed out, Jacob is the logical choice for Bella. He's normal (relatively speaking), and much safer for Bella than a clan of vampires.

However, if you think about it, Bella was already tied to the vampires for three books, and she was deeply involved with the Cullens and their secret. As Alison said, Edward brought Bella too far into the vampire world for her to easily cut off all connections with it. If she had dumped Edward and gone with Jacob, the Volturi would still be after her because she was in on their secret. And then what would've happened? The wolves (with the help of the Cullens, no doubt) would have to fight the Volturi to save Bella. In addition, the possibility of Jacob imprinting on someone else would always be in the back of both his and Bella's minds. Bella could easily have ended up like Leah. And what would have happened to Edward? It's not likely that he would get over Bella and move on; his story would need to be told as well. All in all, if Bella made the snap decision to ditch Edward and go with Jacob, the series would be just as intriguing.

○○○
which event in the Twilight saga was the most surprising?

Bella's pregnancy

Dawn, 26, California

Bella getting pregnant was a twist I did not antici-pate. Of all the events that occurred in the book—the Volturi, Bella becoming a vampire with powers, Jacob being a shape-shifter—the pregnancy took me com-pletely by surprise.

Paige, 16, Texas

In the entire Twilight saga, the moment when Bella realized she was pregnant was most surprising. Throughout all the books, not once does Stephenie Meyer hint that vampires have the ability to have children, especially with humans. Readers hoped that Bella would stay with Edward (I'm a Team Edward fan) but I never even thought that Bella and Edward could have a real family together. Of course, I was ecstatic when I found out, and I was terrified. I could predict the outcome of some situations in the books, I never believed that could happen, so Bella's pregnancy came as a surprise.

Jacob imprinting on Renesmee

Rachel, 15, Georgia

The event that was the most surprising in the Twilight saga was Jacob imprinting on Renesmee. I honestly don't think anyone saw Renesmee coming, as Stephenie Meyer had mentioned that vampires can't reproduce, and then after the shock of Renesmee, suddenly Jacob was imprinting on her. I know I went back and read that part twice to make sure I wasn't confused, and I'm sure many other readers did as well. At that point in *Breaking Dawn*, I was expecting Jacob to end up with Leah. When Renesmee came around and he imprinted on her, I was the most shocked I have ever been while reading the Twilight saga.

Bristol, 17, Texas

Jacob imprinting on Renesmee was the most surprising because it signified the end of the saga, and it left every pair ending happily ever after. Bella and Edward were finally together for eternity, and Jacob imprinting meant that his love for Bella, the cause and justification of so much strife and 1,000 pages of emotional stress, would no longer be a source of conflict for him, Edward, and Bella. In essence, with that fight won, all that was left was that coveted romantic flourish at the finale, the conclusion that all Team Edward and Team Jacob fans could harmoniously approve of.

Edward leaving Bella

Dayi, 19, Georgia

I'd have to say that, for me, Edward leaving Bella was the most surprising event in the Twilight saga. When I read *Twilight* I fell in love with their love. I loved the characters as they were and was happy to read more of their awesome story in *New Moon*. I cannot describe how disappointed I was when I turned the pages and saw the names of the months depicting how long Bella was without Edward. I may or may not have tossed the book across my room. Sorry! In truth, I never imagined that Edward would leave her, because I believed he loved her as much as Bella believed he did. I was shocked that Stephenie Meyer would leave Edward out of the book as much as she did. But this way, we found out more about the characters' personalities and got to know Bella better. Not to mention the fact that the werewolves wove their paths so intricately with Bella's because of Edward's desertion.

THE FINAL CALL

As many shocking events as there were in the Twilight saga (Edward leaving Bella, Bella's pregnancy, and the birth of Renesmee, to name just a few) I was floored when I read that Jacob had imprinted on Bella's baby. *Breaking Dawn* was filled with surprises, and yet when I got to the end of Jacob's book, I just couldn't believe what was happening. In fact, it didn't totally sink in until Bella's realization of the fact in Chapter 22. For the entire series, fans are led to believe that vampires and werewolves are sworn enemies and that their relationships will never be amicable. I was also convinced that Jacob was never going to imprint after Bella broke his heart. So how exactly did Bella's best friend end up imprinting on her half-vampire child? I was just as shocked as everyone else!

○○○
should Breaking Dawn have ended with a fight?

Yes!

Rachel, 15, Georgia

Breaking Dawn should have ended with at least the beginnings of a fight. There was so much buildup in *Breaking Dawn* that led to absolutely nothing, and I think that's what disappointed fans the most. Everyone reading *Breaking Dawn* had this adrenaline going as they waited for a battle scene, and that adrenaline went nowhere, unless it fueled the disappointment the fans had in the series' conclusion. Without a fight, the happy-ending scene seems cheesy and cliché, almost like the cute little family gathered around sipping coffee at the end of their struggle, much too happily-ever-after and overused. If *Breaking Dawn* had ended with a fight, or even a death, the happiness at the end would have seemed sweet or sad instead of cliché and boring.

Elisabeth, 24, Illinois

In all honesty, by the time I got to the end of *Breaking Dawn*, and of course the whole series, I really wanted a fight. I was geared up for one. We had followed Bella and all of her plans to keep Renesmee safe, as well as the misdirection of Alice and Jasper leaving, the vampires training, and Bella coming into her own as a vampire. By the time I got to that point, I was ready. Then, when it did not happen, it felt anticlimactic. I found myself wondering why I had spent all that time going through the motions. Looking back, I understand that we needed to see what Bella was willing to do to keep her family safe, but it was still an extremely anticlimactic end to the entire situation.

No!

Andrea, 21, North-Rhine/Westphalia, Germany

I don't think it would have been a good idea to end *Breaking Dawn* with a huge fight between the Volturi and the Cullens. I'll admit that it is a bit of a letdown to have nearly half of the book building up to this final confrontation and then resolve everything peacefully. But, as I believe Stephenie Meyer said at some point, this final battle would have resulted in the deaths of many of the characters that readers have come to love throughout the four books. It would simply not have been realistic to have the Cullens and their friends fight the Volturi with their whole watch to back them up and have all the "good" characters survive—even with all the magnificent talents such as Bella's shield or Edward's mind reading. And how could *Breaking Dawn* possibly have ended on a happy and positive note with, say, half of the Cullen family, their friends and the wolf pack dead? Each of the characters has their own personality and special traits that make readers like them and relate to them, and the death of any number of them would have cast a shadow over the happy ending that people feel the characters deserve.

Besides, it is the Cullens' (and especially Carlisle's) philosophy to live as peacefully as possible, and after all the trouble they have gone to in order to be good people, it would not be consistent with their characters to have them slaughtering the Volturi as long as there is another way to solve the problem. So many books end with a final battle and heavy casualties, and it is a nice change to have a book where the characters find a way to end the confrontation through passive resistance and cleverness. This is essentially in keeping with the overall vibe of the Twilight saga, which sets it apart from your average vampire book.

In conclusion, I would say that a battle would certainly have been more exciting after the long buildup, but that, portrayed realistically, it would have taken away the perfect ending and the crucial differences between the Twilight saga and other vampire-fantasy stories—and that is, to my mind, more important than a fight scene.

Dayi, 19, Georgia

Breaking Dawn should not have ended with a fight. If that had happened, to keep the story realistic (or as realistic as a vampire love story can be), Stephenie Meyer would have had to kill a few important characters. And even though that is how life sometimes is, it would have ruined the books and greatly disappointing for thousands of fans. A fight would only have led the series down a more difficult and gloomy path. The ending is perfect as is.

THE FINAL CALL

When I first read *Breaking Dawn*, the ending disappointed me. Like many fans, I was caught up in the whirlwind of events before the concluding chapters, and I was looking for a very dramatic ending to wrap it all up. So naturally I was let down by the lack of a fight at the end of the book. I wanted something big, something grand. After everything that had happened in the series, it just seemed too simple for the Cullens and the Volturi to talk things over and find a resolution.

However, after reading some fan responses, my opinions have shifted a little. Many Twi-hards said a fight would have gone against the Cullens' principle of living a peaceful life. They also pointed out that it would have led to something inevitable—the deaths of many vampires and werewolves, possibly those that we have grown to love.

A painful as a fight would have been, I still stand by my argument that *Breaking Dawn* should have concluded with a showdown (but maybe not as adamantly as I did before). The buildup throughout not only the last book but the entire series made anything less than a fight seem anticlimactic. As Rachel stated, the conclusion of *Breaking Dawn* seemed almost too cheesy and cliché; everything worked out perfectly, and the vampires walked away without any harm. I was thrilled to see the entire Volturi and Cullen families (plus the wolves) finally meet face-to-face. I wanted to see which clan was really the strongest, who had the more potent powers, and who would outshine the other in combat. The absence of a fight disappointed me and many other Twilighters around the world.

○○○
what would've happened if Bella were the vampire and Edward were the human?

Rachel, 14, Illinois

I think the biggest thing that we all can agree on about this question is that if Bella were a vampire, she never would have gotten pregnant in *Breaking Dawn*. This means Jacob wouldn't have imprinted on Renesmee, and the Volturi would never have come. For the rest of the story, it depends on how you look at it. If Bella had been the vampire, would she have been a Cullen? Would she normally drink human blood? Would Edward have had any family or friends? If Bella and Edward's roles were reversed, with nothing changing other than those two characters, things wouldn't play out the same way. Rosalie would never have been so scornful of Bella, and Jacob Black would've seemed like a nonexistent speck on the windshield. Would the book have been told from Bella's point of view, or Edward's? Would there have been another character added into the mix that was like Bella's Jacob? Perhaps someone "safer" for Edward than Bella was? The questions are limitless, and the possibilities infinite. If Bella were the vampire and Edward the human, the entire course of the series would've changed, and personally, I don't feel it would have been as successful.

Rachel, 15, Georgia

If Bella were the vampire and Edward were the human, it would be hard to know what would happen because Bella would lose the little personality she had if she were originally a vampire. She would never have been clumsy, Edward wouldn't have been mystified that he couldn't read her mind because, as a human, he wouldn't be able to read anyone's. Also, Bella never would have developed maternal tendencies because there would be no Renesmee. If it had been the story of Edward, a friendless, clumsy, Phoenix boy moving to Forks, we can't even guarantee that Bella would be attracted to him, as he would have no mysterious draw to her. And, how could we guarantee that Edward's blood would be special to Bella?

THE FINAL CALL

The entire plot of the Twilight saga is based on the story of a mortal girl, Bella Swan, who falls in love with an immortal vampire, Edward Cullen. Edward thinks his mind-reading abilities are limitless until he meets Bella. She is the only being, mortal or immortal, whose mind he can't penetrate. Bella never thinks she could be sucked into a world of vampires and werewolves until she meets Edward. Before that she was just a normal girl living a perfectly normal life in Phoenix, Arizona.

So what would've happened if things were flip-flopped—if Bella were the vampire and Edward were the human? For the sake of simplicity, let's assume that almost everything else stays the same. Bella (the vampire) moves from Phoenix, the Cullens (still vampires) reside in Forks, but Edward (the human) doesn't know about their secret. I think we can all agree that things would be drastically different, maybe even to the point of Bella and Edward not being attracted to each other. Of course, she would know of Edward, maybe even become friends with him, but anything beyond that is iffy.

Bella would no doubt pick out the fact that the Cullens are vampires and probably attach herself to them. Jacob Black's role in the series would be significantly reduced since he wouldn't be in love with the vampire Bella. There would be no love triangle, no rogue vampires trying to hunt down a human, and certainly no half-vampire baby in the end. If Bella were the vampire and Edward were human, the Twilight saga would be missing crucial plot points and be less intriguing.

○○○

Are the comparisons between the Twilight saga and the Harry potter series fair and justified or are they misguided?

They are misguided!

Rachel 15, Georgia

The comparisons between the Twilight saga and the Harry Potter series are completely misguided because the only things these series have in common are midnight release parties and Robert Pattinson in the movies. Harry Potter is a series written about magic and adventure and good versus evil, while Twilight is about love and what love can overcome. They were written to prove completely different points, and although they are both great series, they have huge fan followings because they are so different. Harry Potter and Twilight rip-offs are a dime a dozen, and if Twilight were comparable to Harry Potter, it would never have the tremendous fan following it has today.

Taylor, 16, Wisconsin

Having the Harry Potter series compared to the Twilight series gets under my skin and makes me so furious every time I hear someone bashing one or the other "just because." Personally, I love the Twilight saga more than any books under the sun, but Harry Potter is great too. Plus, the two series are nothing alike! You can't go around comparing vampires and werewolves to wizards and witches! The subjects and plots are completely different, and the characters' personalities have really nothing in common with each other. I don't know why there's this huge debate about them. It's an opinion thing, in my eyes. Twilight will always be better for me, because that's just the way I am. It's the way I perceived it. My cousin is huge into Harry Potter but still likes Twilight. I don't get why some people like to contrast the two, and it drives me insane. I love Twilight. I like Harry Potter. They are two very different things. Stop comparing and start enjoying, you know? It's hard to find good books like these every time you walk into a book store or library.

Dayi, 19, Georgia

In some ways, the comparisons between the Twilight saga and the Harry Potter series are misguided, mainly because they are about two completely different worlds. Stephenie Meyer did not write this story to become famous, so she should not get heat about trying to be a sensation like J. K. Rowling is. Both stories have their merits, fans, and nonbelievers. I absolutely love the Harry Potter books, and Harry Potter and Twilight are both wonderful. I think it is awesome that they are sometimes compared, because Twilight has had just as much, if not more, success than Harry Potter. This just adds to the hype and excitement surrounding these two sagas.

Basically, there is enough room in the world for both the vampire love story and the wizarding world, and they should not be said to be in any sort of competition against each other. The comparisons are mostly misguided except for the success of each one. Most everyone loves one series or the other, and many people, including myself, love both, while some crazy people and do not care about either one. They just need to let these stories live on, and we fans will take care of the rest.

THE FINAL CALL

We've all seen the news reports on TV, in magazines, or online comparing the Twilight saga to the Harry Potter series. While most fans greatly support both series, comparisons between the two tend to anger them. For starters, they claim that the two stories have nothing to do with each other. One is a vampire romance while the other is a fantasy adventure involving witches and wizards. Fans believe the "competition" makes it sound like there can only be one dominant book series in existence, which is totally not true. I personally am a very big fan of Twilight (obviously) as well as Harry Potter, but unlike most fans, the comparisons between the two don't make me want to scream. I can see where journalists get the idea to analyze the similarities between the two series. They're more alike than you think. For one thing, both the Twilight saga and the Harry Potter series are worldwide phenomena popular among teenagers. They both focus on supernatural beings and fantasy worlds where magical talents and abilities help save the day. Twilight of course is a love story, and although Harry Potter lacks a major romantic aspect, isn't the overarching theme "love conquers all"? To me, the comparisons between the two are justified, and even though most fans despise the thought of it, there are solid reasons to make connections between the two wildly popular series.

○○○
should Bella have been transformed into a vampire?

Yes!

Rachel, 15, Georgia

Bella should have been turned into a vampire because otherwise what would the story lead to? Bella growing up and loving Edward and then getting old and dying and Edward killing himself shortly after? Jacob would probably try to move on from Bella as soon as she was much older than he was, so you'd lose the Jacob aspect of the story if Bella weren't transformed. Also, it just wouldn't be interesting having to hear Bella beg Edward to transform her throughout an entire book or series of books. Bella turning into a vampire was the only route the story could have taken since Bella and Edward admitted their love in the meadow in *Twilight*.

Dawn, 26, California

Yes! Bella had to turn into a vampire in order to fully be with Edward. By her becoming a vampire, Bella and Edward solidify their love and save each other. If Bella had stayed human, Edward would have committed suicide upon her death. In order to fully appreciate the intensity of their love and for them become a symbol of everlasting love, their physical relationship had to also become immortal.

Hannah, 16, England, UK

This is a hard and detailed question. Throughout the saga, I did always hope for Bella to one day become a vampire. So when it finally happened, I was left a tad disappointed by the way in which it occurred. I think Stephenie took a major risk in bringing a child into the story, as a child changes everything. A child changes other characters' maturity and tests how much "change" the readers can cope with. I think it all depends on what you feel attracts you to Bella and Edward's relationship. For me it's the tension, some sexual, but mostly due to the huge difference between them—Edward is a vampire and Bella is a human.

Bella as a human starts off as an independent girl. She's not looking for anything, yet she feels the need to make others happy. I think maybe if others are happy, she can see herself at peace too. Obviously Bella changes from *Twilight* to *Eclipse*. She becomes a lot stronger mentally and can make her choices more easily. We still see this Bella in the beginning of *Breaking Dawn*. She appears nervous on her wedding day, and she's still intimidated by Edward's beauty (as are we). But as a lot of readers have noticed, Bella's character completely shifts onto another level as soon as she becomes pregnant. This affects a lot.

We find out that Bella wants the child, though we've had no previous indication of Bella having a maternal instinct. She's still very young, so as the pregnancy leads to Bella turning into a vampire, and I have to be honest—I don't like it. Although she's still insecure about herself and will never see herself as equal to the Cullens and Edward, she is. I think in the previous books, we all Bella and Edward as complete opposites, yet they needed each other. Now that Bella is a vampire, Bella and Edward are equals. Both are strong individuals, and both have the same ability to rip someone's head off. Strange. What I found most disturbing was the scene in which Bella first hunts. My image of Bella is weak, fragile, feminine, and petite, so I guess that scene took me by surprise even though it was to be expected.

My answer is yes, Bella should have been turned into a vampire. But I think she should of have been turned into one a different way, without bringing a child into the series. Of course this would lead to no imprinting and no fight scene at the end of *Breaking Dawn*. I would just like to think that if Bella were to become a vampire without a child, maybe her character would still hold what we've always known Bella to be: just an everyday girl who comes across a future she's never dreamed of having.

THE FINAL CALL

From the moment Bella sees Edward, her life takes a turn that alters her fate forever. She falls in love with a vampire, and the only way to remain with him is for her to become one of his kind. From the beginning of the saga, I, along with many other fans, saw it as inevitable that Bella would eventually be transformed into a vampire. Bella wants to be part of the Cullen family—not as a human—and she adamantly makes up her mind at the end of *Twilight* that she wants to be changed. It's the only way she can spend eternity with the love of her life. On top of that, the saga's happy ending and peaceful resolution would not have been possible if Bella had stayed human. Too many "what ifs" and unanswered questions would have been left dangling in the air. Would Bella and Edward find a way to stay together? What would happen when Bella started to age? Bella's transformation saved all of these questions from being asked. She could now spend the rest of ... well, forever with Edward, which is what she wanted the day she fell in love with him. The final verdict? Bella should definitely have been transformed into a vampire.

ooo
also available
from ulysses press

LOLcat Bible: In teh beginnin Ceiling Cat maded teh Skiez an da Erfs n stuffs

Martin Grondin, $12.95

Those adorable and wildly popular LOLcats translate classic Bible stories into absurdly hilarious LOLspeak.

Mugglenet.com's Harry Potter Should Have Died: Controversial Views from the #1 Fan Site

Emerson Spartz and Ben Schoen, $14.95

Digging into every reference in all seven books, the Mugglenet .com founders present fun debates about everything Potter.

The Unofficial Harry Potter Vocabulary Builder: Learn the 3,000 Hardest Words from All Seven Books and Enjoy the Series More

Sayre Van Young, $16.95

Easy and entertaining definitions for the more difficult words in all the Harry Potter books.

Vampires Don't Sleep Alone: Your Guide to Meeting, Dating and Seducing a Vampire

Elizabeth Barrial & D. H. Altair, $12.95

A deadly serious guide for anyone looking to seduce the most dangerous—and exciting—of romantic playmates.

What Will Happen in Eragon IV: Who Lives, Who Dies, Who Becomes the Third Dragon Rider and How Will the Inheritnce Cyle Finally End?

Richard Marcus, $12.95

Professional critic Richard Marcus draws on an intimate knowledge of the first three Eragon books to craft spot-on predictions for the final installment.

To order these books call 800-377-2542 or 510-601-8301, fax 510-601-8307, e-mail ulysses@ulyssespress.com, or write to Ulysses Press, P.O. Box 3440, Berkeley, CA 94703. All retail orders are shipped free of charge. California residents must include sales tax. Allow two to three weeks for delivery.

about the author

Michelle Pan is the owner of BellaAndEdward.com, one of the largest Twilight saga fansites on the web. She founded the site in October of 2006 when she was just 13 years old. With almost four years of online history, BellaAndEdward.com continuously strives to provide fans of the Twilight saga with the latest news on the series and its films. Michelle has been interviewed by many media outlets including ReelzChannel.com, *Business Week*, and her local news station, KXAN. She has had the opportunity to attend the *Twilight* and *New Moon* movie premieres and interview many important cast and crew members, including author Stephenie Meyer. Now a junior in high school, Michelle divides her time among school, band, and her Twilight fansite. She lives in Austin, Texas.